Cleveland, Oh. Wiggins

History of Decatur, Illinois

its resources, advantages for business, and attractions as a home, with a

brief sketch of its manufactories, prominent business and professional

men

Cleveland, Oh. Wiggins

History of Decatur, Illinois
*its resources, advantages for business, and attractions as a home, with a brief
sketch of its manufactories, prominent business and professional men*

ISBN/EAN: 9783337179519

Printed in Europe, USA, Canada, Australia, Japan

Cover: Foto ©Andreas Hilbeck / pixelio.de

More available books at **www.hansebooks.com**

HISTORY

OF

DECATUR, ILLINOIS,

ITS

RESOURCES, ADVANTAGES FOR BUSINESS, AND ATTRACTIONS AS A HOME,

WITH A

BRIEF SKETCH OF ITS MANUFACTORIES, PROMINENT BUSINESS AND PROFESSIONAL MEN. ALSO, A COMPLETE CLASSIFIED BUSINESS DIRECTORY.

COMPILED AND PUBLISHED BY
WIGGINS & CO., CLEVELAND, OHIO.

———

DECATUR, ILLINOIS:
1871.

INTRODUCTORY.

The following pages are presented to the public, for two reasons :

First, To show to parties not already acquainted with our city and surroundings, but who contemplate a change of residence, and may be seeking a good location for manufacturing or business enterprise, the superior advantages which this city presents.

Second, To present a historical sketch of the city and its surroundings, together with a correct and complete classified business directory.

WIGGINS & Co.,

Publishers.

HISTORY OF DECATUR.

EARLY HISTORY AND SETTLEMENT.

By C. H. Fuller, Esq.

"Macon county was formed out of territory attached to Shelby county, and originally included within its limits nearly all of the counties of DeWitt, Piatt and Moultrie, and was created by an act of the Legislature, January 19, 1829. John Fleming, Jesse Rhodes and Easton Whitton were appointed commissioners to locate the county seat, which, when located, was to be called Decatur.

"The first County Commissioners' Court was held at the house of Jas. Ward, four miles south of this city, on the 19th of May, 1829. Benjamin Wilson, Elisha Freeman and James Miller composed the court, with Daniel McCall as clerk. The next meeting of this Court was held at the same place on the first day of June, 1829. At that Court the following order was passed: 'Ordered that B. R. Austin, County Surveyor for the county of Macon, be and he is hereby required to lay out the town of Decatur, in said county, after the form of Shelbyville,' &c. The Commissioners appointed to locate the county seat reported at this meeting that they had located the same on the northeast quarter and east half of section fifteen, township sixteen, two east. The first sale of lots was on the 10th of July, 1829.

"The first white person that settled in the county was William Downing, who located on the south side of Sangamon river in the year 1820. Two years later, Leonard Stevens and family moved to the county and settled about three miles northwest of this place, on Stevens' creek.

"The first house erected in the town was built by James Renshaw, on lot three, block three, old town; and the next by P. D.

2

Williams, on the lot where the hardware store of Close & Griswold now stands.

"The first meeting of the Trustees of the town of Decatur was held on the fifth day of November, A. D. 1836."

THE CITY OF DECATUR,

The county seat of Macon county, is situated within 14 miles of the geographical centre of the State of Illinois, and has a population of about 10,000 inhabitants.

Its present railroad facilities are not surpassed centrally within the State, and it will, when railroads now under contract and actual building are completed, rival its neighboring city of Indianapolis as a centre—the iron bands of which, yearly add to the welfare, financially and socially, of *its* people, and must, as a natural result, so prove to Decatur—whose rapid growth since the first railroad touched here in 1854, has proven in the result now firmly established, with a successful future admitted by its sister cities.

No city in the west is more healthy, or better supplied with water for domestic and manufacturing purposes, or fire protection. The unlimited liberality and public spirit of its citizens in the support of schools, churches and like public benefits, speak for its people the elements of success in creating and perpetuating the vital growth of a western city, educationally and morally. Commercially, the health in markets is "A. No. 1." No disastrous effects from any financial storm, or the wave of civil war, have made lasting impressions upon the Court Records of the county. The municipal taxes are, by comparison, lighter than a large majority of western cities, never having exceeded to the year 1871 the rate of one per cent. on an assessed value of about 66 per cent. of the actual value. The city debt is $55,000, payable $20,-000 in 1879 and $35,000 in 1891, the debt being created for permanent improvements; a portion of which $35,000 must, of necessity, become almost self-liquidating at maturity in the revenue derived therefrom, viz: *Water Works.*

The city contains about 40 miles of streets and 60 miles of side walks. Most of the side-walking being made of wood, requires for present some yearly expenditure for repairs, and to meet the increasing demands for new walks on the newly opened streets, and homes made thereon. The replacing of wooden walks is in many instances made of stone, which becomes, with our railroad facilities, not an expensive change, when durability is considered.

The pages following will show to the reader (under appropriate headings,) the various resources, business and advantages, with statistics interesting, and modestly hoped convincing, as to why Decatur must become a large commercial and manufacturing centre, and which you are respectfully invited to peruse, compare, judge and act as to your individual pleasure and profit, and with views to an addition of " live elements" essential to mutual benefits in the " *coming* and *being*."

MUNICIPAL GOVERNMENT.

BOARD OF TRUSTEES.

1836.—Richard Oglesby, President. Trustees: Wm. T. Crissey, G. R. White, *Wm. Webb, Thomas Cowan, †H. M. Gorin, Henry Butler, Landy Harrell. †Andrew Love, Clerk; James Carter and Wm. Webb, Constables.

1838.—†Joseph Williams, Henry Snyder, Presidents. Trustees : James Renshaw, James F. Montgomery, George R. White, Henry Prather. Edmund McClellan, Clerk; Richard Oglesby, J. P. Hickcok, Treasurer ; John S. Adamson, Assessor ; William Radcliff and Thomas Cowan, Supervisors ; J. H. Elliott, Constable.

1839.—Trustees : William T. Crissey, S. B. Dewees, J. M. Fordice, ‡James F. Montgomery.

† Resigned.   * Died.   ‡ It does not appear from the record that these last named trustees ever met, but that there was an election held on the 6th day of May, 1839, under a special act incorporating the town of Decatur, at which election another board was chosen.

1839.—Kirby Benedict, President. Trustees: John S. Adamson, Thomas Cowan, Samuel B. Dewees, Jesse H. Elliott, Wm. T. Crissey, Thomas H. Read. H. M. Gorin, Clerk; George R. White, Treasurer; H. Prather, Assessor and Collector; G. W. Gilbrath, Zebulon Cantrall and William Webb, Constables.

1840.—Joseph King, President. Trustees: Henry Goodman, William Cantrill, B. F. Oglesby, David Wright, John G. Speer, David E. Ralls. H. M. Gorin, Clerk; G. R. White, Treasurer; I. C. Pugh, Collector; William Webb, Constable.

‡ 1841.—Thomas P. Rodgers, President. Trustees: J. H. Elliott, D. E. Ralls, G. R. White, Henry Goodman, Benjamin R. Austin, J. D. Tait. J. S. Post, Clerk; J. H. Read, Treasurer; Joseph Stevens, Assessor and Collector; Wm. Webb, Constable.§

1846.—David Krone, President. Trustees: Elijah Krone, Joseph Kauffman, Michael Elson, Thomas H. Read. E. B. Hale, Clerk; G. A. Smith, Constable.§

1854.—William Prather, President. Trustees: William J. Stamper, William S. Crissey, Joseph King, Thomas H. Wingate. B. H. Cassell, Clerk.

1854.—Thomas H. Wingate, President. Trustees: William S. Crissey, William Martin, Elias Tanner, John Ricketts. B. H. Cassell, Clerk; H. Churchman, Constable.

1855 —Thomas H. Wingate, President. Trustees: A. L. Kellar, J. R. Gorin, William S. Crissey, William Martin. B. H. Cassell, Clerk.

CITY COUNCIL.

*1856.—John H. Post, Mayor. Aldermen: Frank Priest, 1st Ward; E. O. Smith, 2d Ward; †J. R. Gorin, S. P. Ohr, 3d Ward; J. J. Ballentine, H. Taylor, 4th Ward. C. C. Post, Clerk and Attorney.

---

‡ This was the last meeting of the Trustees of the town of Decatur for five years.
§ The record of the proceedings of the Town Trustees from 1846 to January, 1854, are lost, consequently there is no means of ascertaining who the Trustees were during that period.
* An election was held for city officers, under a special charter, on the 7th of January, 1856.

1857.—William A. Barnes, Mayor. Aldermen: George Goodman, Joseph Mills, 1st Ward; H. B. Durfee, George Dempsey, 2d Ward; A. T. Hill, John P. Post, 3d Ward; Israel B. Gring, Geo. Wessels, 4th Ward. J. P. Boyd, Clerk and Attorney.

1858.—James Shoaff, Mayor. Aldermen: Joseph Mills, J. B. Trull, 1st Ward; H. B Durffee, Isaac D. Jennings, 2d Ward; John P. Post, Samuel F. Greer, 3d Ward; George Wessels, O. Powers, 4th Ward. S. S. Goode, Clerk and Attorney.

1859.—A. T. Hill, Mayor. Aldermen: James Simpson, J. L. Mansfield, 1st Ward; John W. Bear, M. Hayworth, 2d Ward; Samuel F. Greer, William Lintner, 3d Ward; O. Powers, J. C. Benton, 4th ward. S. S. Goode, Clerk and Attorney.

1860.—Sheridan Wait, Mayor. Aldermen: James Simpson, S. S. Hale, 1st Ward; E. McNabb, William J. Scanlan, 2d Ward; William Lintner, Peter M. Wykoff, 3d Ward; J. C. Benton, John L. Peake, 4th Ward. J. R. Gorin, Clerk and Attorney.

1861.—E. O. Smith, Mayor. Aldermen: F. Priest, long term, Chas. A. Tuttle, short term, 1st Ward; James Millikin, Wm. J. Scanlan, 2d Ward; †W H. Bramble, P. M. Wykoff, 3d Ward; Joel C. Benton, long term, Wm. A. Barnes, short term, 4th Ward. J. R. Gorin, Clerk and Attorney.

1862.—Thomas O. Smith, Mayor. Aldermen: F. Priest, D. H. Elwood, 1st Ward; James Millikin, Lowber Burrows, 2d Ward; Henry Goodman, W. H. Bramble, 3d Ward; Joel C. Benton, Bensel Henkle, 4th Ward. J. R. Gorin, Clerk and Attorney.

1863.—J. J. Peddecord, Mayor. Aldermen: D. H. Elwood, David S. Hughes, 1st Ward; James Millikin, Lowber Burrows, 2d Ward; Wm. H. Bramble, Henry Goodman, 3d Ward; John Ullerich, Benson Henkle, 4th Ward. J. R. Gorin, Clerk and Attorney.

1864.—J. J. Peddecord, Mayor. Aldermen: C. A. Tuttle, D. L. Hughes, 1st Ward; M. Y. Givler, James Millikin, 2d Ward; M. Fostmeyer, J. G. Starr, 3d Ward; Benson Henkle, long term, T. B. Albert, short term, 4th Ward. K. H. Roby, Clerk and Attorney.

1865.—Franklin Priest, Mayor. Aldermen: Charles A. Tuttle, Charles H. Fuller, 1st Ward; M. Y. Givler, Wm. J. Usrey, 2d Ward; M. Fostmeyer, E. A..Barnwell, 3d Ward; †Benson Henkle, S. T. Trowbridge, 4th Ward. K. H. Roby, Clerk and Attorney.

1866.—Franklin Priest, Mayor. Aldermen: †Charles H. Fuller, S. F. Hawley, 1st Ward; W. J. Usrey, E. McNabb, 2d Ward; E. A. Barnwell, M. Fostmeyer, 3d Ward; G. Howell, short term, H. Muller, long term, 4th Ward. † A. B. Bunn, Clerk and Attorney.

1867.—John K. Warren, Mayor. Aldermen: †S. F. Hawley, Joseph Mills, 1st Ward; E. McNabb, 2d Ward; M. Fostmeyer, J. R. Gorin, 3d Ward; H. Muller, B. F. Dodson, 4th Ward. C. H. Fuller, Register.

1868.—Isaac C. Pugh, Mayor. Aldermen: D. P. Elwood, Joseph Mills, 1st Ward; L. L. Haworth, S. Burrows, 2d Ward; M. Forstmeyer, J. R. Gorin, 3d Ward; B. F. Dodson, H. Prather, 4th Ward. C. H. Fuller, Register.

1869.—Wm. L. Hammer, Mayor. Aldermen: D. P. Elwood, D. S. Shellabarger, 1st Ward; L. L. Haworth, J. L. Libby, 2d Ward; M. Fostmeyer, G. S. Simpson, 3d Ward; H. Prather, W. F. Busher, 4th Ward. C. H. Fuller, Register.

1870.—F. Priest, Mayor. Aldermen: †E. M. Misner, D. S. Shellabarger, 1st Ward; Benj. Dill, *E. McNabb, 2d Ward; G. S. Simpson, M. Forstmeyer, 3d Ward; W. F. Busher, E. Harpstrite, 4th Ward. C. H. Fuller, Register.

1871.—E. M. Misner, Mayor. Aldermen: Joseph Mills, *Wm. J. Myers, 1st Ward; Benj. Dill, E. McNabb, 2d Ward; M. Fostmeyer, Wm. H. Bramble, 3d Ward; E. Harpstrite, Wm. Gabler, 4th Ward. C. H. Fuller, Register.

---

† Resigned.   * To fill vacancy.

RAILROADS.

By F. N. EWING, Esq.

A full history of the various railroads passing through, or terminating at Decatur, would .require more space than could be allowed in a work of the nature of this, and more time and patience than the general reader ought to be supposed to possess. This article will be confined to the few main points which will be of use in giving to the public a bird's eye view of the origin, progress, and present state of the railroad facilities of this place, with a fair statement of the probable completion of roads in the future.

THE ILLINOIS CENTRAL RAILROAD.

A company was chartered in 1836, to construct a road over nearly the same route now occupied by this road, and the route was surveyed; but the project failed at that time for the want of means.

An act of Congress, granting lands to the State of Illinois, for the purpose of aiding in the construction of a great railroad, with a branch, through the central part of the State, was approved Sept. 20th, 1850. The Illinois Central Railroad Company was incorporated by the Legislature of this State in 1851; and the lands granted by Congress were conveyed to the Company as soon as they had complied with the conditions of the charter. In a few years the entire road was finished and in full operation from Cairo, at the junction of the Ohio and Mississippi rivers, to Dunleith, on the latter river, a distance of four hundred and fifty-six miles; and the branch from Centralia to Chicago two hundred and fifty-three miles.

This road, by the facilities afforded for travel and transportation of produce, gave an impulse to improvements that are marvelous to all, who saw the country twenty years ago, and see it now. Then, there were wild wastes of prairie as far as the eye could reach, without a sign of human life, where now every acre of land is under cultivation, and clothed over with towns and cities. But while the credit, in a large measure, of developing the resources of the central portion of the State, is due to this road, other roads followed, which afforded outlets in other directions.

THE TOLEDO, WABASH AND WESTERN RAILWAY.

The Great Western Railroad was chartered in 1853 ; and after several amendments and consolidations, was finished and in good working order, under its present name, viz : Toledo, Wabash and Western Railway, from Toledo, on Lake Erie, to Quincy, on the Mississippi, a distance of four hundred and seventy-six miles. This road, which crosses the Illinois Central Railroad at Decatur, nearly at right angles, passes through the finest portions of this State and the State of Indiana, and into the State of Ohio, and touching Iowa at Keokuk. Beside the great facilities for travel and trade by means of this road, East and West, it brings to our door the fine timber, coal, and stone with which the States east of us abound, and is rapidly developing the rich coal fields, over which the road passes in this State. So much is the benefit in this regards felt, that wood is cheaper to-day in Decatur, with a demand more than doubled, than it was a few years ago. And there are large manufactories of agricultural implements, furniture and iron, here, which could not exist without this road.

	MILES.
The Main Line is	476
St. Louis Division (from Decatur to St. Louis)	106
Keokuk Branch	43
Hannibal Branch	50
Pekin Branch (from Decatur to Pekin)	65
Pittsfield Branch	6
Moberly Branch (in Missouri)	68
Total	814

Of these 814 miles there are in Illinois :

	MILES.
Main Line	226
St. Louis Branch	106
Pekin Branch	65
Keokuk Branch	43
Hannibal Branch	50
Pittsfield Branch	6
Total in Illinois	496

THE DECATUR AND EAST ST. LOUIS RAILROAD

Was chartered in 1867, and soon afterwards put under contract and pushed to completion to the bank of the Mississippi River, opposite the city of St. Louis, a distance from Decatur of one hundred and eight miles. By means of one of the most magnificent bridges in the world, now building, the trains will pass over into the city. This road is said, by persons accustomed to traveling, to be one of the finest roads in the country, and one of the most pleasant to ride on. It is under the control of the Toledo, Wabash and Western Railway Company, and is run in connection with that road.

The next road which I shall notice is

THE DECATUR AND STATE LINE RAILROAD,

because this road forms a continuation of the Decatur and East St. Louis road in an almost perfectly air-line route between St. Louis and Chicago, passing through Decatur, near the middle, and will be shorter by twenty-seven miles, than any other route between those cities. Twenty-five miles of the road are under contract, and there is every reason to believe the whole road will soon be under contract, and finished during the year 1872; so that in twelve months trains will run through from St. Louis, on the Mississippi, to Chicago, on Lake Michigan, without delay or change.

THE PEKIN, LINCOLN AND DECATUR RAILROAD,

which connects this place with the Illinois river at Pekin, in chronological order, comes before the last mentioned road; for it is now so near completion that the cars will be running the whole length of the road, which is sixty-seven miles, in less than thirty days from this time, the 27th of September. The work is all done, except a few miles on the prairie north-west of Stephens' creek.

THE DECATUR, MONTICELLO AND CHAMPAIGN RAILROAD

was incorporated a few years ago, and part of the grading done; but work ceased for want of means. Arrangements are now being made by some gentlemen to finish the road in a short time; and thus give Decatur another route to Chicago by way of Champaign, there connecting with the branch of the Illinois Central.

THE DECATUR AND MATTOON RAILROAD

was chartered in 1861; but owing to the civil war nothing was done towards building the road till a little over a year ago; when it was taken hold of by parties who are rapidly pushing it to completion. The grading is all done from Mattoon to a point within about twenty miles of Decatur; and the ties and iron down. This road is a continuation of the Mattoon and Grayville road, which will be extended to the Ohio river at Evansville. The route will run through a fine prairie country in this State, and a splendid timber country in Indiana; and bring this city, by another line, into direct connection with the trade of the southeast and south.

DECATUR AND PARIS RAILROAD,

which will connect with the St. Louis, Alton and Terre Haute railroad, is finished, and the cars are running more than half the distance from Paris to this place, and will be pushed to completion in a short time.

INDIANA AND ILLINOIS CENTRAL RAILROAD.

This road, which is to be an air-line route from Decatur to Indianapolis, was begun a number of years ago, but on account of counter influences, the work was interrupted from time to time. Arrangements are now about completed, by which it is confidently expected the road will be finished in the course of the next year. This road is of no less interest to Decatur than any other road, either passing through or terminating here. For, beside the connection it gives this place with all the roads leading from that great railroad centre, north, east and south, it passes through some of the finest timber in the State of Indiana, and over beds of the finest coal in the western country, and through immense bodies of as fine building stone as there is in the world.

PEORIA, ATLANTA AND DECATUR RAILROAD.

The act of incorporation says, "this road shall be run by a south-easterly direction to the town of Atlanta, and thence in the same direction to Decatur." Some work has been done on the road, and the president promises its completion at an early day.

Thus it will be seen that Decatur, which is near the geographical centre of the State of Illinois, is, by the four railroads now finished, and the five or six, which will be finished during the year 1872, brought into direct connection with all the great markets of the United States. By the Illinois Central connecting at Mendota with the C., B. & Q. Road, and by the Decatur and State Line Railroad direct, it is connected with Chicago; thence by the great line of lakes with the north and east. And by the same road terminating at Cairo, there is a direct route to New Orleans, both by rail and river; and northward to Dubuque with the great North-western and Pacific routes of travel. By the Toledo, Wabash and Western Railway, running east and west, and East St. Louis Road running southwest, and the Pekin and Decatur Road running northwest, we have connections through St. Louis, Quincy, Keokuk and Pekin with the great routes of river and rail travel south, southwest, west and northwest; and thus by more direct routes reaching the Pacific Ocean. And by way of the Toledo, Wabash and Western Road, the Indiana and Illinois Central Road, the Decatur and Mattoon, extended through Grayville to the Ohio river, Decatur has easy and direct routes of travel and transportation through Indianapolis, Evansville and Louisville, Ky., east, southeast and south.

AGRICULTURAL RESOURCES.

By Dr. H. C. Johns.

This county contains 580 square miles of territory, lying immediately south of the fortieth parallel of latitude, and is, geographically, the centre county of the State. It is also the centre of the great corn and grass belt of Illinois. The surface is generally level, but sufficiently undulating for all the purposes of drainage, without extensive artificial means. The Sangamon river passes through the county from northeast to southwest, with a belt of timber from three to five miles wide. Several small streams, from the northern and southern border of the county, empty into the Sangamon, making, altogether, a better supply and better distribution of water and timber than any other of the prairie counties of the State. A description of the soil, however elaborate, would convey but a limited idea of its productive capacity, without mentioning somewhat in detail the quantities of the crops produced. To say that it is a rich, black loam, containing sand and lime, with a sub-strata of rich, yellow, porous clay, is but repeating what is said of most alluvial soils. The crops successfully grown, with the average yield per acre, will enable those unacquainted with the locality to properly estimate its agricultural resources.

Corn is the grand staple of the prairie lands of the West, and, in this county, is one of the peculiar successes of the farmer. An average of fifty bushels to the acre is the rule for all well cultivated fields. Equal in importance to the corn crop is the grass crop. Two important varieties are indigenous to the soil, viz: blue grass and white clover. The other varieties, red clover, timothy, red top, must be sown, but all yield abundantly, and are an important element of the wealth of the county.

Wheat is one of the staples of this county. The climate is such that both the fall and spring varieties may be successfully raised, and results entirely satisfactory to the husbandman are annually realized from this crop. What is said of wheat, may be truly said of rye, barley, oats and buckwheat. In addition to the consumption of these grains, they make an important part of the export trade of this county. Hemp and flax are as natural to the soil as corn and grass, and yield the farmer a fair return for the labor bestowed.

This county is not surpassed by any in the State as a fruit growing region. Apples are produced in great abundance and perfection, with an occasional crop of peaches. The small fruits, grapes, cherries, strawberries, gooseberries, blackberries, raspberries and currants, are hardy, and yield as much per acre as any other county in the State. Potatoes, turnips, cabbage, sweet potatoes and melons, are grown in great perfection in all parts of the county. The following may be stated as the average yield per acre of the crops that are annually produced in the native soil without the use of manures:

	Bushels per acre.
Corn	50
Wheat	20
Rye	25
Oats	50
Barley	40

Buckwheat... 50
Flaxseed.. 10
Potatoes.. 150
Turnips... 250
Onions.. 100
Hay..One and a half tons.

The artificial manures of commerce have not been used. Where barnyard manure has been tried double the above crops have been realized. Fertilizing the soil will be left to future generations, as many fields in this county have been cultivated for forty years without materially diminishing its productive capacity. The combination of level surface, soil, climate, timber, water, variety of products, ease of culture, abundant yield of crops, and general adaptation to the wants of man, makes the county a rich and desirable inheritance for an industrious and enterprising people.

COMMERCE AND MANUFACTURES.

By H. B. DURFEE, Esq.

The commerce of this city is mainly based upon her manufactories. Take away the flouring mills, rolling mill, oil mill, pump factory, furniture factories, engine factory, boiler factory, implement factories, foundries, machine shops, planing mills, wagon and carriage factories, &c., &c., and the commerce of Decatur would be even less than when but a few years ago, one yoke of oxen did the switching of the two great railroads then passing through our city from the four cardinal points of the compass. And but for the manufacturing establishments that have sprung up in the past few years, that same yoke of oxen might still be lazily wandering amid the few cars our commerce would demand. But our work shops have changed all this, and at the present time, two good locomotives find constant employment in distributing loaded cars, and cars to be loaded, to the various workshops and manufacturing establishments, and making up trains that are almost hourly leaving our depot. And while the ever rumbling trains and the shrill whistle of the locomotives are constant reminders of the active commercial and manufacturing interests of our city, yet in all these things we are but in our infancy.

To utilize the increased facilities for manufacturing and commercial intercourse about to be afforded by the numerous lines of railroads now being constructed to this point, our citizens are disposed to contribute liberally toward the best interest of the community by encouraging manufacturing industry.

Capital, well managed in manufacturing any of the various articles of necessity, or even luxury, cannot fail to find a remunerative market in the rich country to the south of us, to the north of us, to the east of us, to the west of us

The more extensive and varied our manufactures, the more important do we become as a commercial centre. The increase of capital in our manufacturing interests, will continue to attract the mechanic and laborer, and at the same time fix the attention of capitalists, who are always quick to appreciate the advantages of a prosperous community. We have but to be true to ourselves, and we cannot fail to realize immense advantages from the several new railroads which will be completed to our city within the next few months.

CHEAP HOMES AND DISTRIBUTIVE CENTRE.

BY J. K. WARREN, ESQ.

The price of land for all purposes, in and around Decatur, has been, and is, held at very moderate figures, considering all the advantages of the place.

Building lots, within easy distance of the business centre, being procurable at reasonable prices and on easy terms, has induced nearly every comer to purchase, improve and make a home of his own, and thereby realize the comfort, as well as the poetry, of resting under the shadow of his own vine and roof-tree. Thus it is, that for a town of nearly ten thousand people, Decatur has very little dwelling property held subject to rent. Consequently, the character of the inhabitants is of a much higher order than if it had more of a floating population.

The marvelous rapidity with which new railroads have been projected and put under construction in the past few years throughout the country, but especially in the west, is such that the term "Railroad Centre" has become so hackneyed, that but little attention is now paid to the claim that is appropriated by so many aspiring villages securing a few lines of railroads.

But amid the wonderful net-work of iron that is to form THE means of communication, transportation and travel over this great country, but few points will really be able to claim equality with Decatur as a centre. Having now six lines completed, and six more under construction, making twelve lines radiating, as spokes from a hub, to all points of the compass, Decatur, prospectively, can well claim to be considered of no less importance as a "distributive point" than Indianapolis, St. Louis or Chicago.

BUILDING MATERIALS.

BY MILLS & HARRY, BUILDERS.

BRICK, SAND, STONE, LIME AND LUMBER.

In the materials above named, Decatur can claim as a *chief*, the excellence in *brick*. Within easy distance of delivery, of manufactured material, clay banks abound, and labor and skill in the making, provide an abundance of substantial building material of that class, of superior quality.

SAND of good quality, and easily obtained, is found on the banks of the Sangamon river, and elsewhere, and in inexhaustable quantities.

STONE is not of a natural deposit near the city, and wants are supplied by means of railroads.

LIME. The result of Lime Stone, necessarily is not obtained except by similar facilities.

LUMBER is in abundance, of hard wood qualities, at the rate of $20 to $25 per M. delivered.

The *materials* not naturally products, are supplied by railroads, and cars loaded at Michigan Pineries and Indiana Timber

Regions convey their cargo direct to Decatur without breaking bulk. The supply of stone and lime at quarries and kilns within the State and adjacent thereto, by like facilities of railroads, is fully equal to any demand; and while the immediate vicinity of Decatur is not enriched by natural products of soft wood, lumber, stone and lime, yet with cheap transportation and a healthy competition purifying in its results in that direction, building in the aggregate, taking into consideration all material entering into the same, is, and can be done in Decatur at as low figures as cities more closely situated and having that local building advantage in all classes of material not fully supplied here.

To the person of ample purse, it makes but small difference when taste is gratified by sight and ease in domicile; but to the young professional man or mechanic of moderate means, starting in life, and seeking a home in a live western town, it means *dollars and cents, earned by toil*, and to be expended in the comforts of a home: and when it be said that because Decatur has not ALL advantages in building material at hand, that it necessarily must be an expensive place to build in, the proof will not justify the conclusion. Practical results settle the matter; and from carefully compared estimates of buildings erected of similar character in Decatur and elsewhere, Decatur cost is not in advance of sister towns and cities.

It is not in the province of this article to represent " *Building Material* " as present, when not existing, but to clearly set forth what the individual locating and building *may depend on*, and thereby dispense his means in building a "*home*," that great desideratum of all, according to his taste and purse as advantageously pecuniarily, here as elsewhere, in central localities.

GENERAL WATER SUPPLY.

By C. H. Fuller.

The Sangamon River running from a northeast direction, passes a point due east from northeast corner of city, on a line running southwest, about three miles distant. A short distance south and east of corporate limits it bears by a graceful bend almost due west, and passes a point south of centre of city, about one mile distant, when it bends gently to the northwest, thus almost encircling the city at no point in distance exceeding three miles, and reduced on south side of the city to about one mile. At the nearest practicable point near river above and east of natural city sewerage deposit, the city has located the pumping house, engines, etc., to which from the river by means of conduit pipe 16 inches diameter, is lead to a pumping well, and from thence lifted and forced through iron mains 12, 8, 6 and 4 inches internal diameter, through the central portion of the city, and hence to Railroad Crossings, Rolling Mills, etc. Street hydrants are placed at given points for fire protection. Domestic and manufacturing supply is made by tapping mains whenever desired. The water is lifted and forced through mains, by means of stationery engines at pumping works, with sufficient power to answer all purposes, especially so for fire protection, by a direct connection at hydrants with hose, thus obviating any necessity for steam or hand fire engines, and saving yearly a large expense thereby, and rendering *every hydrant an engine wherever located*, when connected with hose and pipe.

The city has expended in pipes, engines, etc., (already in operation) about 15,000 dollars, and the contract to complete at river 35,000 dollars, making a total of 50,000 dollars, which machinery is capable of lifting and forcing (if required) one million gallons of water every 24 hours, sufficient in its capacity to furnish a population of forty thousand inhabitants with water for all purposes required. The Sangamon River water, except at its extreme low stages, is soft, and not impregnated with lime deposit of any importance to make it objectionable, but preferable for steam or manufacturing purposes. For domestic or culinary purposes it is not anticipated to be preferred by all, to good limestone water procured from wells, of which there is an abundant supply, and easily obtained by digging from 25 to 40 feet ; but for general use, viz: fire protection, manufacturing purposes, sanitary purposes, fountains, hotels, livery stables, etc., it meets all possible demands, and is in its effect and advantages equal to a stream of living water quietly pursuing its way through the streets of the city, with the advantage of not being made a recepticle for street and vault washing, the natural reservoir of a city's uncleanliness, as the sequal proved by Chicago river coursing its streets until otherwise diverted.

This important item of water supply to a city, especially so to all manufacturing and railroad interests, puts Decatur on an equal footing with inland river cities as to water demand and supply, being fully equal to any and all requisition in the natural growth of the city. It is carefully estimated that an additional expenditure of $50,000 would so place water through the streets within the city, as to protect with 2000 feet of hose, every domicile within the corporate limits from fire, and admit of its daily use by a population of 30,000 people.

The works now under contract are to be in successful operation by the 1st day of November, 1871, but will undoubtedly in present forwardness of work, be anticipated in time. With this artificial means of a WATER SUPPLY, direct from a fountain at all times equal to demand, the citizens of Decatur rest content, so far as its uses are required, and with justifiable pride point out this permanent improvement as one worthy of its cost, and beneficial to all without exception, and especially so to manufacturing interests, seeking investment and location at a centre, touched by radiating lines of railroad accessible to market here or hence. And with this WATER SUPPLY and all other advantages of a business centre, educational, religious and social privileges, and a beautiful and healthy home, no city in Illinois can, with argument, in truth designate a location more desirable on all grounds considered, than THE CITY OF DECATUR, the "Indianapolis of Illinois."

GAS SUPPLY.

BY J. K. WARREN, ESQ.

Decatur was seen by "Gas Light" for the first time in November, 1868, and has as complete and well ordered set of Works for their size, as any place can boast of, and of sufficient capacity to meet the demand for years to come. The cost of the Works and extensions up to the present time is over $60,000.

Street mains now extend a distance of one and a half miles southwest from the Illinois Central Depot, embracing in their course the business portion of the city as well as many of the dwelling blocks, and extensions continue to be made as rapidly as the prospect of consumption justifies.

The price of Gas nominally is $4 50 per thousand cubic feet, from which 50 cents per thousand is deducted for prompt payment monthly. A further reduction is made upon a scale graduated to the amount consumed per month, as low as $3 00 per thousand. In fact, no place in the State is supplied with Gas Light at any lower rates than Decatur.

HEALTH.

By Dr. — CHENOWETH.

"Filth and over-crowding, short supplies of water and ærial impurities," recognized local causes of sickness, do not exist in Decatur.

Being on elevated ground, seventy-five feet above the Sangamon river, which approaches within half a mile of the city on the south, it is naturally so well drained that very little labor and expense will make the sewerage perfect.

In the early settlement, and until the growth of the town caused the removal of contiguous ponds and sloughs, ague and other malarial fevers prevailed, but now no western city is more exempt from this class of diseases. The mortality in Decatur in the month of June, 1854, when the population did not exceed one thousand, was greater from miasmatic diseases alone, than it has been during the past three months (with a population of ten thousand) from all diseases.

The water supply, which is abundant, independent of the Water Works now being constructed, is obtained from wells sunk to gravel beds or quicksands, which underlie every part of the city from twenty to fifty feet below the surface. The water is of good quality, free from mineral or other impurities, and is generally limestone or "hard water," but there are a few wells of "soft water" near the railroad depot.

In the south part of the city, on Mr. J. Imboden's property, is an artesian well, which possesses very decided medicinal qualities. Dr. J. V. Z. Blaney, of Chicago, made a chemical analysis of the water, as follows:

"One Litre of water taken. Whole amount of solid matter found by evaporation to complete dryness, .483;.291 grammes in 1 Litre of water, which is equal to 27.116,251 grains in 1 W. S. gallon of 221.780 cubic inches.

"This solid matter consists of chloride of Magnesium .0474.506 grammes in 1 Litre, or 2.66197866 grains in 1 gallon,

Sulphate of Lime	.0365190 grains in 1 Litre, or	2.0487159 0	grains in 1 gallon.
Carbonate of Lime	.02008595 "	"	11.60481795	"	"
Silica	.175	"	"	9.8175	"	"
Iron and Alumina	.0175	"	"	.98175	"	"
Total	.4833291	"	"	27.11470251	"	"

"Carbonic Acid Gas uncombined and held in solution, 70.44 cubic inches."

The city will doubtless be a resort for invalids in search of health, not only on account of the excellent quality and medicinal virtues of this water, but also because it affords most desirable sanitary surroundings.

EDUCATIONAL.

BY PROF. E. A. GASTMAN.

PUBLIC SCHOOLS.

DECATUR HIGH SCHOOL.

Our city has five school buildings; the high school, of which four rooms are used for the seating of pupils; the 1st Ward, all of the rooms being in use; the 2d Ward, most of them at present in use; the 3d Ward, all used; 4th Ward all used. The buildings are all in good repair, and furnished with most modern improvements in way of ventilation, seating, heating, &c., and cost completed as follows:

High School, complete	$35,000
1st Ward School, complete	15,000
2d Ward School, complete	15,000
3d Ward School, complete	20,000
4th Ward School, complete	14,000

The schools of Decatur have always received the most liberal support of its citizens, whose aim has been to afford not only advantages such as are usually found in the common public schools, but if possible, to attain a higher standard, and that there might not be a necessity for any of its citizens to send their children away from parental over-sight and care. And such has been the success attained, there has not been a *felt need* in the way of independent educational institutions.

The course of study, as will be seen on the following pages, is the most complete and thorough, comprising not only all the branches usually taught in public schools, but also many of those belonging to a classical education.

The schools of the city are all under the charge of experienced and intelligent teachers, to whom the most liberal salaries are paid, much higher than many of its sister cities.

The schools are managed by a Board of Education, consisting at present of Wm. L. Hammer, Henry B. Durfee and Samuel F. Greer. The officers of the Board are Wm. L. Hammer, President; J. R. Gorin, Treasurer; E. A. Gastman, Clerk and Superintendent. Twenty-nine teachers are employed in the schools the present year:

HIGH SCHOOL.—E. A. Gastman, Miss M. M. Sargent, Miss Mary W. French, Miss Emily H. Cotton. Primary Department—Miss Sarah E. Allen, Miss Jennie E. Durfee.

FIRST WARD.—Mr. David Bigelow, Mrs. Alice E. Slocumb, Miss Alice M. Betzer, Miss Mary A. Perry.

SECOND WARD.—Miss M. W. Carson, Miss Maggie Kerr, Mrs. P. E. Foulke, Miss Carrie Jameson, Miss Sallie Roe.

THIRD WARD.—Miss C. M. Parker, Miss Mary E. Grunendike, Miss Annie E. Haskell, Miss Maggie Sollars, Miss Rachel Cook, Miss Fannie Johns.

FOURTH WARD.—Miss Mary Wilder, Miss Anna Magee, Miss E. M. Beswick, Miss Kate Stickel.

JONES' SCHOOL.—Mrs. N. W. Coleman.

COLORED SCHOOL.—Mr. E. R. Adams. Training Teacher—Miss Lizzie Leeper.

The following "Courses of Study" will show the work proposed to be done in the schools:

WARD SCHOOLS—COURSE OF STUDY.

	PRIMARY DEP'T.		INTERMED. DEP'T.		GRAMMAR DEP'T.		
GRADES........................	I.	II.	III.	IV.	V.	VI.	VII.
Readers....................	1st	2d	3d	4th	Int.	5th	5th
Spelling.........................	X	X	X	X	X	X	X
Writing.........................	Slate	Slate	X	X	X	X	X
Arithmetic.................. {	Oral	Oral	Felter I.	Felter II.	Felter II.	Ray's III.	Ray's III.
Geography......................	Oral	......	Ele.	Ele.	Int.	Int.	......
Grammar........................	......	......	......	......	......	X	X
History U. S....................	......	......	......	......	......	......	X
Object Lessons.................	X	X	X	X	......	......	......

☞ Each Grade corresponds to a Scholastic Year.

TEXT BOOKS USED IN THE WARD SCHOOLS.

Hillard's Readers and Tablets,
Payson, Dunton & Scribner's Copy Books,
Ray's Arithmetic, 3d Book,
Seavey's Goodrich's History,
Guyot's & Mitchel's Outline Maps,
Boston School Tablets,
Worcester's Speller,
Felter's Arithmetic, 1st and 2d Books,
Guyot's Geographies,
Quackenboss' Guide to Composition,
National Tablets,
Greene's Introductory Grammar,
The Nursery,
Worcester's and Webster's Dictionaries.

HIGH SCHOOL—COURSE OF STUDY.

FIRST YEAR.

FIRST TERM.	SECOND TERM.	THIRD TERM.
English Grammar and Anal. Physical Geography, Arithmetic, Latin Grammar.	English Grammar and Anal. Physical Geography, Arithmetic. Lat. Gram. and Reader.	Civil Government, Review U. S. History, Book Keeping, Lat. Gram. and Reader.

SECOND YEAR.

Zoology, Physiology, Algebra, Cæsar.	Geology, Natural Philosophy, Algebra, Cæsar.	Botany, Natural Philosophy, Algebra, Cæsar.

THIRD YEAR.

FIRST TERM.	SECOND TERM.	THIRD TERM.
History.	History.	History.
Astronomy.	Political Economy.	Rhetoric.
Geometry.	Geometry.	Trigonometry.
Virgil.	Virgil.	Virgil.

FOURTH YEAR.

FIRST TERM.	SECOND TERM.	THIRD TERM.
English Literature,	Eng. and Am. Literature,	Etymology,
Chemistry,	Chemistry,	Reviews,
Cicero.	Mental Philosophy,	Moral Philosophy.
	Cicero.	

Drawing, Penmanship, Spelling, Reading, Declamation and Composition through-out the course, as may be deemed necessary.

Pupils wishing to prepare for college, will commence Greek at the beginning of the third year. Latin is optional, and pupils studying it will omit such other studies as may be deemed best by the Principal.

TEXT BOOKS USED IN THE HIGH SCHOOL.

Walton's Written Arithmetic,
Greene's Grammar,
Warren's Physical Geography,
Hillard's Sixth Reader,
Worcester's Speller,
Tenney's Natural History,
Gray's Botany,
Wilson's Outline History,
Youman's Chemistry,
Allen's Latin Grammar and Lessons,
Bryant & Stratton's Book-Keeping,
Davies' New Elementary Algebra,
Tenney's Geology,
Cutter's Physiology,
Steele's Philosophy,
Davies' Elementary Geometry,
Olmsted's Astronomy,
Davies' Trigonometry,
Andrews & Stoddard's Latin Grammar,
Hanson's Latin Prose Book,
Haven s Mental Philosophy,
Wayland's Moral Philosophy,
Guyot's Maps,
Worcester's & Webster's Dictionaries.

Below will be found a brief summary of school statistics for the year 1870–1:

Whole number of different pupils enrolled	1,882
Number of male teachers employed	3
Number of female teachers employed	25
Average number belonging	1,436.5
Average daily attendance	1,357.7
Per cent of attendance	94.5
Number of tardinesses during the year	1,895

Highest salary paid male teachers	$1,500
Lowest " " "	450
Average " " "	1,050
Highest salary paid females	700
Lowest " "	315
Average " "	490
Salary paid superintendent	1,800
Cost per pupil for tuition	11.42
Entire cost per pupil	19.48

CEMETERIES.

By J. R. Gorin, Esq.

The stockholders of the Cemetery Association, in Decatur, organized under the general law of the State, on the 27th day of March, A. D. 1857, by electing William Martin, Sr., president, Nathan W. Tupper, treasurer, and John Ricketts, David L. Allen and Daniel C. Lockwood, directors. The name given to the Association, and by which it is designated, is "The Decatur Greenwood Cemetery."

The Cemetery is situated south of and adjoining the city. Since the organization in 1857, the grounds have been tastefully laid out, and many who have purchased lots have ornamented them, and fitted them up in a style which makes the place look cheerful and attractive. The grounds have become quite a resort for the citizens, especially for those who have friends buried there. For the present beautiful arrangement of the grounds, and the improvements made thereon, we are largely indebted to Hon. Henry Prather, deceased, who was, at the hour of his death, and had been, for several years previous, president of the Association, and who devoted a great deal of his time in devising means to beautify and adorn the grounds, and make them more attractive. The grounds are still being beautified under the present management. Alexander T. Hill, president; Wm. L. Hammer, John Ullrich and Henry B. Durfee, directors, and J. R. Gorin, secretary and treasurer.

VINEYARDS.

By Theodore Hildebrandt, Esq.

The choicest and most grateful of all fruits, the Grape, is grown here quite extensively. Ever since its introduction from Asia into Europe, it has kept pace with civilization. There are about 300 acres in cultivation, 150 of which are in bearing, and the business has been very remunerative to vineyardists. Of the 300,000 vines grown, one-half are Concords, one-quarter Catawba's and the rest the various kinds, such as Delaware, Roger's Hybrids, Iona, Clinton and innumerable new varieties put into the market annually by Horticulturists. The yield of wine in 1870 was about 500 barrels, one-half of which was made by the Decatur Wine Company, whose product compares favorably with that of older makers in older wine districts. The time is not far distant when Central Illinois will not be compelled to import wine from other States and countries, but will largely export, and give to our people a good wine as cheap as the poor people of the old countries get it. There are yet hundreds of acres of fine river bluff lands in the vicinity of Decatur, well adapted to the growth of the Grape, which can be bought very cheap. The soil of these bluff lands is peculiarly rich, and just such as the vineyardist always looks for but seldom finds, and only awaits the labor of experienced men and a little capital to give hundreds remunerative employment and pleasant homes.

FAIR GROUNDS.

By O. BRAMBLE, Esq.

The Decatur Fair Grounds, situated one-half mile south of the city limits, were first laid out in 1857, by a stock company, and most of the present improvements were made while under its control. In 1868 the grounds were given to Macon county. They have an area of forty acres, the entire grounds being a natural grove, cleared only sufficient to make room for the necessary buildings and sheds, and affords shade of unusual beauty and extent.

An eight foot tight board fence encloses the grounds. There are six springs within the enclosure, which furnish water to an unlimited extent and of the best quality. The principal buildings consist of a large amphitheatre that has accommodations for 5,000 persons ; Farm Product Hall, 40x100 ; Mechanical and Industrial Hall, 40x60 ; A Fine Art Hall, (octagon,) 40 ft.; Cattle Stall accommodations for nearly 500; also Pens for 500 Hogs.

The Illinois State Fairs have been held here for the years 1863–64, and 1869–70.

4

These grounds are thought, by all who have visited them, the most beautiful and best for fair purposes of any in the United States, and considered by most of the patrons of our State Fair, as an appropriate place for its permanent location.

PUBLIC LIBRARIES AND SOCIAL ORGANIZATIONS.

LADIES LIBRARY ASSOCIATION.

This organization, as indicated above, is under the exclusive management of the ladies of the city. It is in a flourishing condition, and is considered one of the best and most permanent institutions of the place. Besides opening to the public an excellent circulating library, this association is the organized medium for securing lectures from abroad.

The Circulating Library is open every Saturday, from 1 o'clock until 5 o'clock, P. M., for exchange of books. Any person may become a life member of the Association by the payment of $25, or an annual member on the payment of $3. And any member shall be entitled to all the privileges of the Association.

THE CONCORDIA CLUB.

Such is the name of an association existing in our city. Its purposes are the promotion of the literary and social amusements. It was founded in the fall of 1868, by a few of the most prominent German citizens, and although at first intended exclusively for Germans, it has become so popular, and the influence has been so strong, as to change the programme materially, and the Club counts amongst its members, not only the prominent Germans, but some of the most prominent of Americans. The Germans' social spirit, aided by the advanced ideas of their American fellow citizens, have established the Association upon a most permanent footing, socially as well as financially.

The Club Room offers entertainments for lovers of tragedy or comedy, lovers of music, or those that desire the more retired pastime of reading. Newspapers and periodicals from abroad, as also the most prominent literary journals of the country, are kept; while the singing club, although as yet in its infancy, offers much towards the fulfillment of the most sanguine expectations. The instrumental entertainments, presided over by the accomplished Prof. Goodman, are all that can be desired.

The association truly deserves the support of all liberal minded citizens, and we bespeak for it a happy and prosperous future.

— ◆ —

CHURCHES.

BAPTIST.

First.—Was constituted September 14, 1843, with twelve members. The successive pastors have been: H. W. Dodge, Moses Lemen, B. Carpenter, C. H. Gates, N. Alvord, J. N. Tolman, B. F. Thomas, S. G. Miner, F. M. Ellis, F. G. Thearle and S. F. Holt. The present number of members is 180. The Sunday School has 200 members; Geo. F. Wessels, Superintendent. Their house of worship, a brick edifice, sixty feet by forty, on the north-east corner of Water and William streets, was dedicated December 27, 1857. It is expected it will soon give place to a more commodious and elegant building, one better suited to the present strength and tastes of the Society. The present officers of the Church are: S. F. Holt, Pastor; Geo. Wood, M. Y. Givler and D. Moses, Deacons.

Rolling Mill Chapel.—Erected by the Baptist Church in 1871, at a cost of about $2,500. Sabbath School has 150 members; Ira Harris, Jr., Superintendent.

Antioch, African.—Was organized 1858, with 14 members. Has a comfortable house of worship on South Main Street, near Bramble's Grove. At present without a pastor.

CATHOLIC.

St. Patrick's.—Organized 1854. Present church building erected 1863, and is a handsome brick edifice, with sittings for about 800 persons. The interior is finished in most excellent taste, and is very attractive. Present Pastor, Rev. R. A. Welch. Number of members about 300 families, or 1,500 persons. Sunday School

200 pupils. Parochia School, 100 scholars, under charge of P. A. O'Brian. Theresa Academy, under care of this church, now closed, it is expected will be open in November, under charge of Ursaline Sisters, of New York.

CHRISTIAN.

Organized 1833, with 12 members Rev. Ira Mitchel, present Pastor. Present membership about 150. Number scholars in Sunday School, 100; William Shocky Superintendent. The house of worship is a plain one, and is quite too small for present congregations.

CHURCH OF THE UNITED BRETHREN IN CHRIST.

Organized by Rev. James Neighbarger, A. D. 1854, with six members. House of worship, a plain brick building, erected in the year 1857. Corner North Main and Cerro Gordo Streets. Val ued at $3,500. Parsonage, same block, valued at $2,000. Total, $5,500. Present number of members in Church, 110; number in Sabbath School, 125. L. Field, Pastor, G. Smelsby, Treasurer. At present, no Superintendent of Sabbath School.

UNIVERSALIST CHURCH.

On Prairie Street, between Main and Water. Organized 1856; 80 members. Building and lot valued at $6,000. Rev. S. F. Gibb, Pastor. Sunday School organized 1856; attendance 75. Volumes in Library, 400. D. L. Bunn, Superintendent.

CHURCH OF GOD.

The Church of God, in Decatur, was organized May 1st, 1857, by Elder A. J. Fenton and assisted by Elder John Winebrenner, consisting of ten members. The following year the Church erected present house of worship at the corner of North Water and Cerro Gordo streets. The present church has fifty members, with Elder M. S. Newcomer as pastor. The Sabbath school has about one hundred members.

PROTESTANT EPISCOPAL.

St. Johns', located on North Water street, near Eldorado; was organized in 1855. Wardens, Cyril Fuller and James Forester; Lober Burrows and William S. Quinlan, Vestrymen; Lober Burrows, Treasurer; Wm. S. Quinlan, Secretary.

LUTHERAN.

German, church building corner Wood and Edward's streets.

METHODIST EPISCOPAL.

The Methodist Episcopal Church was organized in the year 1831. The Rev. Ashel E. Phelps was preacher in charge of what was then called " Salt Creek Circuit." In 1838 the name changed to " Decatur Circuit." In 1854, Decatur became a station, and Rev. Reuben Andrus was the first stationed minister. A small frame building situated on lot 7, block 2, original town of Decatur, was for many years their place of worship; this was succeeded in 1852, by a brick edifice 40x60 on the corner of East Prairie and North Water streets, and this by the present magnificent edifice, 85x120 feet, on the northwest corner of North Water and William streets, costing when completed $60,000. This edifice was commenced under the auspices of Rev. Levi C. Pitner, preacher in charge, in 1868. The congregation worshipped for three years (the audience room being unfinished) in the lecture room, the completeness of the arrangement of which for Sabbath school purposes is well worthy of note. In June, 1871, Rev. James H. Noble, preacher in charge, a contract was made with Messrs. Mills and Harvy for the building (except frescoing). These gentlemen have had the entire superintendence of the work except as above, from the foundation stone to the top of the main spire, and have faithfully carried out the original design to the entire satisfaction of the officers and members of the Church, and have elicited the praise of all who have examined their work. The frescoing is done in a fine, artistic style, and reflects great credit upon Mr. M. Albyer, the painter. The main spire is 180 feet high, and the smaller one 140 feet high. The audience room will accomodate 1,200 persons. The whole edifice for architectural beauty and convenience of arrangement is not excelled by any structure of the kind in the State. It is massive, and finished in a style of magnificence which makes it an ornament to the city, and reflects great credit upon the contractors and the workmen engaged in the erection. The design is by the late O. S. Kinney, Architect, Chicago. Preacher in charge, James H. Noble; Trustees, Wm. T. Stamper, President; Samuel

F. Greer, Secretary ; J. R. Gorin, Treasurer ; Peter M. Wikoff,
Geo. W. Baker, Dr. Enoch W. Moore, Jno. Imboden, Wm. J.
Condell and Caleb C. Burroughs. Building Committee, John
Imboden, C. C. Burroughs and J. R. Gorin. Present menbers of
Church, 450 ; members of Sunday School, 450 ; Superintendent,
J. R. Gorin.

STAPP'S CHAPEL,

Organized in 1867, as Franklin M. E. Church, with fifty members.
Purchased the site and built the present house of worship, corner
Franklin and Edwards streets, 1868, which, together with the par-
sonage, cost about $35,000. It is one of the most attractive and
convenient churches in Central Illinois, and reflects great credit
upon the architect and builders, the latter—Mills & Harry—residents of the city. Present pastor, H. O. Hoffman. Membership
of the Church is 215. Sunday School numbers 300 ; D. S. Shellenbarger, superintendent.

African.—Organized 1862 with four members present. Membership 62. A. McIntosh, Pastor. Number of Sabbath School
scholars, 50. C. S. Jacobs, Superintendent. House of worship
is on S. Main Street, near Bramble's Grove.

German.—Situated on Edwards, near Union. Rev. Lewis
Herman, Pastor.

FIRST PRESBYTERIAN.

Organized May 1, 1852, with 12 members. Rev. Mr. Pratt,
Pastor. Successive Pastors, Rev. David Manfort, Rev. E. W.
Thayer, Rev. P. D. Young, Rev. F. M. Oviatt, Rev. D. C. Mar-
quis, Rev. Samuel Conn. Present Pastor, Rev. J. E. Moffatt.
Elders, S. S. Malone, Orlando Powers, T. H. Allen, G. E. More-
house, J. H. Lewis, R. P. Lytle. Present membership, 240 ;
Sabbath School, 225. Sabbath School Superintendent, W. T.
Wells.

UNITED BRETHREN.

Corner of Main and Cerro Gordo Streets. Rev. Mr. Fields,
Pastor.

COMPARATIVE TAXATION

OF CITIES OF CENTRAL ILLINOIS FOR YEARS 1870 AND 1871. COMPILED BY C. H. FULLER, CITY REGISTER OF DECATUR, SEPTEMBER 1, 1871.

CITIES.	Population	Value of Assessed Property	Rate Per Cent of Tax Levy—Mills on Dollar	Indebtedness	Annual Interest on Indebtedness	Tax Per Capita	Indebtedness Per Capita	Remarks.
1871. Decatur	8,500	$3,788,740 06	13	$55,000 00	$5,500 00	$5 70	$6 47	Owns Water Works
1871. Peoria	25,787	13,813,218 00	13½	1,082,500 00	83,395 00	7 23	41 97	Owns Water Works
1871. Springfield	18,000	11,102,654 00	18	978,949 72	86,269 90	11 10	54 38	Owns Water Works
*1870. Bloomington	16,000	7,050,000 00	....	225,000 00	21,800 00	7 78	14 08	....
*1870. Jacksonville	15,000	4,582,272 00	....	143,700 00	14,376 00	7 33	14 38	....

* The above data could not be obtained to Sept. 1, 1871, and is therefore made up from Comparative Table prepared and published in History of Joliet, Ill., for 1870.—COMPILER.

MASONIC ORGANIZATIONS.

MACON LODGE, NO. 8.

Geo. W. Bright, W. M.
Wm. Gibson, S. W.
D. T. Sherman, J. W.
N. S. Krone, Sec'y.
Wm. L. Hammer, Treas.
W. W. Foster, S. D.
John Swearingen, J. D.
Henry Hummell, Tyler.

IONIC LODGE, NO. 312.

John Quinlan, W. M.
J. H. Babbitt, S. W.
Cyrus Imboden, J. W.
W. A. Moore, Sec'y.
A. A. Murray, Treas.
J. N. Baker, S. D.
James Durfee, J. D.
Wm. Towling, Tyler.

MACON CHAPTER, No. 21.

A. A. Murray, H. P.
John H. Babbitt, K.
J. G. Starr, S.
N. L. Krone, Sec'y.
J. Quinlan, C. of H.

Geo. W. Bright, P. S.
A C. Carman, R. A. C.
Wm. Gibson, C. of 1st V.
Wm. Martin, C. of 2d V.
M. Y. Givler, C of 3d V.
Henry Hummell, Tyler.

DECATUR COUNCIL, No. 16.

A. A. Murray, G. M.
J. R. Gorin, P. C. W.
D. P. Bunn, D. J.
    Regular meeting first Monday of every month.

BEAUMANOIR COMMANDERY, No. 9

A. A. Murray, E. C.
Robert Green, G.
John Quinlan, C. G.
Geo. W. Bright, P.
J. H. Babbitt. S. W.
M. Y. Givler, J. W.
N. L. Krone, R.
S. F. Greer, N.
Albert Emmerson, S. B.
J. G. Starr, J. B.
Cyrus Imboden, W.
Henry Hummell, C. G.

ODD FELLOWS.

DECATUR No. 65

H. M. Oberndorfer, N. G.
P. J. Shoch, V. G.
N. Edwards, R. S.
Wm. Towling, P. S.
G. W. Baker, Treas.
I. N. Martin, Warden.
A. Meisenhelter, Con.
Geo. Backman, I. G.

CELESTIAL No. 186.

C. P. Hansum, N. G.
R. B. Mohegan, V. G.
H. P. Christie, R. S.

Joseph Gates, P. S.
I. W. Eherman, Treas.
M. A. Albeitz, Warden.
H. B. Durfee, Con.
A. W. Slack, I. G.
J. W. Bear, O. G.

DECATUR ENCAMPMENT, No. 37.

C. P. Housum, W. P.
J. P. Farris, H. P.
S. F. Gibb, S. W.
M. Albeitz, J. W.
Wm. Towling, Scribe.
John W. Bear, Treas.

KNIGHTS OF PYTHIAS.

COLUER DE LEON.

B. K. Durfee, W. C.
J. F. McChain, V. C.
B. F. Dodson, V. P.
W. F. McEwen, R. and C. S.

J. W. Balthus, B.
J. W. Routh, G.
A. H. Varney, I. S.
C. M. Durfee, O. S.
    Regular meeting on Wednesdays of each week.

GOOD TEMPLARS.

CENTRAL STAR LODGE, No. 543.

Wm. Towling, L. D.
D. L. Bunn, P. W. C. T.
C. M. Allison, W. C. T.

Mollie Logan, W. V. T.
Orval B. Gorin, W. S.
—— Bradt, W. F. S.
Wm. Oaks, W. T.
Theo. Coleman, W. M.

MISCELLANOUS.

DECATUR TURNVEREIN.

L. Fell, 1st Spreccher.
Geo. Zeiss, Scriftovart.
L. Schlosser, Schatzmeister.

LADIES LIBRARY ASSOCIATION.

Mrs. A. A. Powers, President.
Mrs. M. K. Hatch, Vice Pres.
Mrs. Dr. I. N. Barnes, Sec'y.
Miss Libby Jack, Cor. Sec'y.
Mrs. A. T. Hill, Treas.

CONCORDIA CLUB.

Joseph Michel, Pres't.
Theo Hildebrant, Vice Pres't.
Henry M. Oberndorfer, Sec.
Berthold Stein, Treas.

GERMAN MUTUAL AID SOCIETY.

C. Amman, President.
John Blakely, Secretary.
John Brant, Treasurer.

OFFICERS OF THE STATE, COUNTY, CITY AND TOWNSHIP.

STATE OFFICERS.

Governor ....John M. Palmer.
Lieut. Governor ......John Dougherty.
Secretary of State....Edward Rummell.
Auditor of State......C. E. Lippincott.
Treasurer of State.........E. N. Bates.
Supt. Pub. Inst......Newton Bateman.

CONGRESSMEN.

Senators, Lyman Trumbull, J. A. Logan.
Rep. at Large, 7th Dist., Jesse H. Moore.

LEGISLATORS.

State Senator........Michael Donahue.

JUDICIAL OFFICERS.

District Judge.........A. J. Gallagher.
District Attorney.....M. B. Thompson.
Clerk Circuit Court...... E. McClellan.

COUNTY OFFICERS.

County Judge.... ....S. F. Greer.
County Clerk........H. W. Waggoner.

County Treasurer.........W. M. Boyd.
Sheriff.................Geo. M. Wood.
Deputy................I. D. Jennings.
Supt. of Schools.........O. F. McKim.
County Surveyor........Geo. V. Loring.
Coroner............ .... M. Y. Givler.

CITY OFFICERS.

Mayor............. ......E. M. Misner.
ALDERMEN.
1st ward....Joseph Mills, J. W. Myers.
2d ward.........Benj. Dill, E. McNabb.
3d ward..M. Forstmyer, W. H. Bramble.
4th ward......E. Harpstrite, W. Gabler.
Register. ....Charles H. Fuller.
Treasurer... ....M. K Hatch.
Assessor...............Fred. J. Smith.
Attorney..................J. R. Eden.
Engineer................G. V. Loring.
Supervisor................. A. Martin.
Marshal....... ....Jno. Haworth.
Deputy Marshal.............J. S. Hewes.
Magistrates. A. W. Hardy, G. Goodman.
FIRE DEPARTMENT.
Hook and Ladder Co., No. 1—B. F. Dodson, Foreman ; I. W. Ehrman, Sec'y.

5

TOWNSHIP OFFICERS IN THE CO.

DECATUR.

Supervisor.............. M. Forstmyer.
Asst. Supervisor.........Joseph Mills.
Town Clerk............. Geo. Goodman.
Assessor................Fred. J. Smith.
Collector.............Jacob H. Miller.
Commissioners of Highways.... Henry
　　　　　Cassell, Jno. H. Ham.
Justices of Peace....M. K. Hatch, A.
　W. Hardy, Geo. Goodman, S. Steele.
Constables....H. Churchman, J. J. H.
　Young, Harvey Mahannah, George
　S. Stoy.

FRIEND'S CREEK.

Supervisor ....John Marsh.
Collector..................V. D. Ross.
Assessor........ ....Frank Turner.
Town Clerk.............J. W. Welton.

LONG CREEK.

Supervisor.................J. B. Myers.
Collector.............Benj. F. Wheeler.
Assessor.................Geo. C. Davis.
Town Clerk .... A. T. Davis.

NIANTIC.

Supervisor.............Sheldon Parks.
Collector............. H. A. Williams.
Assessor.............Newman Roberts.
Town Clerk.............Samuel Zarley.

SOUTH MACON.

Supervisor.............Joel T. Walker.
Collector.............S. C. Attleberry.
Assessor ....Thomas Attleberry.
Town Clerk..........Marion Timmons.

MOUNT ZION.

Supervisor.................Wm. Davis.
Collector..................John Scott.
Assessor..............George A. Smith.
Town Clerk..........Jas. D. Campbell.

BLUE MOUND.

Supersvior...............Robt H. Hill.
Collector.............Jos. M. Pasley.
Assessor.................T. P. Steiner.
Town Clerk.... ....F. H. Coleman.

HARRISTOWN.

Supervisor............. M. G. Camron.
Collector...................J. H. Cox.
Assessor................... A. Eyman.
Town Clerk............. H. C. Masters.

AUSTIN.

Supervisor..........Charles F. Emery.
Collector...........Andrew Hawkyard.
Assessor................Jos. W. Emery.
Town Clerk............Jas. H. Newton.

ILLINI.

Supervisor..............Jos. C. Tucker.
Collector...............Joseph Brown.
Assessor...................J. S. Childs.
Town Clerk.............Chas. Remie.

MARAO.

Supervisor...............Samuel Lowe.
Collector..............Thos. N. Levitt.
Assessor....................A. Wykoff.
Town Clerk...............J. M. Gault.

MILAM.

Supervisor..........George A. Bartlett.
Collector................D. J. Freeland.
Assessor.................John R. Hight.
Town Clerk................ J. M. Kerr.

WHITMORE.

Supervisor...............Joshua Green.
Collector................. A. B. Kuhns.
Assessor................. R. M. Machan.
Town Clerk................S. G. Coal.

HICKORY POINT.

Supervisor..............Alex. McBride.
Collector....................J. R. Hays.
Assessor...................J. R. Moon.
Town Clerk..............Geo. Shaffer.

SOUTH WHEATLAND.

Supervisor...............Hiram Ward.
Collector............... Lewis Morris.
Assessor.............Jos. M. Trobaugh.
Town Clerk............. W. S. Nichols.

PLEASANT VIEW.

Supervisor. ....D. D. Powler.
Collector.................... O. Ulrich.
Assessor...............E. T. Clements.
Town Clerk.................E. House.

OAKLEY.

Supervisor...........Emanuel Rhodes.
Collector................. .. ——. ——.
Assessor................E. R. Alsburry.
Town Clerk.......... .....—— ——.

MANUFACTORIES, MILLS, BUSINESS HOUSES AND PROFESSIONS.

We present here a sketch of all the different manufacturing establishments of Decatur. We would not indicate by this, there are no openings for more of a like character, but to show by the omission of any not enumerated here, *their* more immediate need; and also showing to the agriculturist a prominent inducement to locate where all their wants can be supplied without cost and delay of transportation, and at prices corresponding favorably with eastern markets. We also give a sketch of the most prominent business houses and professions.

DECATUR AGRICULTURAL WORKS.

A joint stock company, organized under the general laws of the State, went into operation in the fall of 1868, under the management of H. B. Durfee, Esq., as general superintendent. These works are amply provided with buildings and machinery, for giving employment to from 200 to 250 men. Their buildings, consisting of foundry, blacksmith shops, machine. shop, wood-workers' shops, paint shops, store houses, &c., occupy five acres of ground immediately east of the Central Depot. During the past year they gave employment to an average of about one hundred men, and during six months of the year, including the winter months, they employed one hundred and forty five men.

The constantly increasing facilities for distributing of their manufactures, coupled with the rapidly growing demand for the peculiarly desirable goods manufactured by them, will soon justify the employment of the largest number of men their extensive works will accommodate.

The leading feature in these works is the manufacture of plows and cultivating implements Among which are, Durfee's Clear Landside Clipper Plow, Sattley Gang Plows, Sattley Sulkey Plows, Sod Plows, the Victor Wheeled Walking Cultivator. They also manufacture wheat drills, corn planters, harrows, barrows, road scrapers, etc.

CENTRAL IRON WORKS.

Early in the spring of 1865, Burroughs & Co. commenced to build what they intended simply as a first class shop for repairing machinery, but their work giving such general satisfaction, a demand arose for the manufacture of mill machinery and steam engines, and they were compelled within two years from their commencement, to enlarge their shops or turn the work away from their door.

Their shops, as then enlarged, consist of brick buildings containing the following rooms : Machine shop, 30x140 ft.; foundry, 50x60 ft.; pattern room, 30x70 ft.; and store room 30x50 ft., with a capacity for working 50 men.

From this time their work continued to increase, from the fact that in adopting patterns for machinery, they chose those which combined strength and utility without clumsiness. All unnecessary weight saved being a saving of money and friction.

In their engines they sought simplicity and durability, and yet did not overlook symmetry. While they did all their work well, they gave extra care to the working parts of their engines, avoiding weight where it was not needed, and adding it where it would increase the strength. The vital part of an engine is in the manner of working steam, and no steam can be economically worked without a good valve, and to this point the best mechanics have given their closest study for many years.

The "Ives' Balanced Slide Valve," adopted by Burroughs & Co., was at the time of its adoption little known, having been patented but a few months before, and its present popularity honors their mechanical judgment in its selection. The valuable points in this valve, and valve motion, are briefly as follows : 1st, Being nearly balanced, little is lost in friction. 2d, Steam packing of valve is always tight, requires no grinding, and will last as long as the engine. 3d, Large ports give free passage to steam. 4th, Valve operating at either extreme end of the cylinder, no steam is lost in side pipes. 5th, Steam may be easily and accurately cut off at any portion of the stroke, so that no more steam need be used than is necessary for the load. 6th, Every part is durable.

Their engines are specially liked in those mills and factories where the greatest possible saving of fuel and perfect regularity of motion, under varying loads, is indispensable. In fact, so well balanced and fitted are they in all their parts, one of their chief excellencies is found in the fewness of the repairs which they require. The best testimony as to their popularity is found in the fact that where one of their engines is introduced there soon arises a demand for more.

Their coal-shaft engines have gained a good reputation, as also their other coal shaft machinery. One of their pumps in the Jacksonville coal mine, having the capacity for the discharge of 600,000 gallons in 24 hours. They also manufacture saw mills, sorghum machinery, house castings, bridge bolts, and almost anything made from iron.

The growth of their business and other manufacturing interests in the city, shows a strong contrast with the time when manufactured articles were all brought from the east. Now the west, at least that portion of it which lies in the valley of the Mississippi, can supply its wants almost within itself, and the time must soon come when the east will have to look elsewhere for its trade.

HAWORTH'S CHECK ROWER.

This invention was first introduced to the public by Geo. D. Haworth, the inventor, in 1869, and has proved to be one of the greatest inventions of the times. The first year two machines were sold, both in Macon county; the following year five hundred were sold, and in 1871, two thousand.

The firm of Haworth & Sons employed about 50 men the past year. The Check Rower is used in all the western States, and gives universal satisfaction.

It can be attached to any and all corn planters now in use, and should be used by every farmer who plants twenty acres of corn.

The advantages are patent to any one who will for a moment consider the value in saving the marking off of the ground in check rows; in saving the weight of a man on the planter, besides his time; but the greatest gain is in the fact that with this machine you can plant the corn the same day the ground is broken up, which gain alone would, in the year 1869, have made millions of bushels of corn for the State of Illinois. It plants with accuracy, making a row of corn that can be plowed both ways with perfect ease.

COOPERS.

There are several cooper establishments here, the two most prominent are under the management of D. Martin and William Whrust, who make nearly ten thousand barrels a year.

FURNITURE.

One of the most prominent manufacturing establishments of Decatur is the Furniture and Pump Factories of Wm. Lintner & Co., located on East Prairie and Broadway streets. This establishment was started by Messrs. Barnes and Lintner, in 1862, who gave their attention to the manufacture of pumps and agricultural implements, employing but five men. The business was conducted at that time on a very small scale, and

continued so until 1866. At this time Mr. Barnes withdrew from the firm, and was succeeded by Wm. Lintner & Co., the present proprietors, who increased the amount of capital and enlarged their facilities, by the erection of the present buildings for a furniture manufactory.

The main building is 108x36 ft., five stories high, and an addition 100x32, three stories high, with an L 99x92, three stories high, beside a building used for drying and storage of lumber.

The interior is arranged with the most modern improved machinery, and every convenience for the workmen, with a due regard to the health and comfort of the men in way of ventilation and protection from dust.

This firm employ at present about 70 men, to whom they pay annually about $30,000. There is about 100,000 feet of lumber used in the pump and furniture departments, and 15,000 feet of veneering. Amount of capital invested in buildings, machinery, &c., is $100,000. The sales amount to over $125,000 per annum.

The furniture made at this establishment is equal to any in the United States, and comprises every grade of chamber, dining room, kitchen or office furniture; and at prices that will compare favorably with that of eastern markets. The pumps are of a superior quality, and have an enviable reputation and large sale throughout the west.

WAGON AND CARRIAGE MANUFACTORIES.

This branch of business is carried on quite extensively in Decatur, there being three large establishments who make the manufacture of wagons and carriages a speciality. There are a number of wagon and blacksmith shops which give considerable attention to new work, as well as general repair business

Messrs. Gahman & Wicks have one of the most complete establishments in the city, and make every description of wagons and carriages, and of a superior quality, as their rapid increase of business bears evidence.

N. Hamsher & Son, have the largest shops, and turn out an immense amount of work in way of fine carriages, buggies, as well as wagons, which are sold through Macon and adjoining counties, and are considered equal in quality and prices, to that of the best eastern makers.

Taylor & Bradley, have also an extensive establishment, formerly carried on by the veteran wagon and carriage maker, Jos. Athons, who still resides in Decatur, and gives some attention to this branch of trade, but mostly to repair business.

PLANING MILL, SASH, DOOR AND BLIND MANUFACTORY.

The Planing Mill and Lumber Yard of Messrs. Elwood & Co., was started in 1865, who by close attention to, and a thorough knowledge of their business, gained for themselves the reputation of being one of the most successful and reliable firms of Decatur. Their mill is furnished with all the usual kinds of machinery found in a first class manufactory. They handle over 200,000 feet of lumber, annually, which is sold at their yard, or made into doors, sash, blinds, &c. They give employment to 22 men, to whom they pay upwards of $13,000 a year. Their annual sales average $100,000 per annum.

WOOLEN MILLS.

The Decatur Woolen Mills were established in 1859, by Messrs. Boyd, Haskell, & Co., the present proprietors. The firm consists of W. H. Boyd, L. C. Haskill & Wm. J. Myers, who, with the assistance of three workmen, constituted the early working force, and run but one machine. Owing to the industry and energy of the proprietors, also the large increase of business, they soon added another machine. In 1868, the establishment was entirely destroyed by fire, and although slightly insured, the firm immediately erected the present extensive buildings. The main building is 142x40 ft., three stories high, with an L 92x86 ft., and run 720 spindles, 11 looms, 2 sets of cards. The present capacity is sufficient to manufacture 90,000 lbs of wool per annum. There is 100,000 yards of flannels, jeans, &c., 20,000 pounds of yarns. Their yearly sales amount to $75,000. The new building is calculated to run double the present amount of machinery, which will be added at no distant day. The mill is under the supervision of Mr. J. Myers, the senior member of the firm, whose thorough knowledge of the business is a guarantee of the future success of the enterprise.

FLOURING MILLS.

The Flouring Mill owned by Mr. Geo. Priest, is on the corner of East Main and the Illinois Central Railroad track; was established in the year 1856, by Henkle & Condit. Mr. Priest becoming a part owner in 1861, and during the present year purchased the entire interest. The building is a large substantial brick edifice, with storage capacity for about 35,000 bushels of grain. The mill has four run of stone, capable of grinding 140 bushels per day. The capital in the building, machinery, &c., is about $32,000. There is ground at this mill about 7,500 bbls. of flour, annually. The sales amount to $100,000 per annum. The products of this mill have acquired a standard reputation, and find a ready sale in eastern markets.

The Flouring Mill of J. M. Raney & Co., was established in 1870, and is located near the T. W. & W. R.W. It has three run of burs, and a capacity for grinding 75 bbls. of flour per day. Capital invested, about $20,000; and sales amount to $100,000 yearly.

D. S. Shellenbarger & Co.'s Mill, on the T. W. & W. R. W., is a fine brick building. Has four run of burs, and a capacity for grinding about 50,000 bus., annually. Has $40,000 capital invested, and its sales amount to $125,000 per annum.

LINSEED OIL MILL.

The Decatur Linseed Oil Mill was established in 1867, and is located on East Main street, near I. C. R. R. It has one set crackers, one set temporary stones, two heaters and two presses. Gives employment to ten men, has a capital of $30,000, and sales amount to $75,000 annually.

BREWERY.

The Brewery Business is carried on quite extensively in Decatur, by Messrs. Harpstrite & Schlauderman. It was commenced in 1856, by Messrs. Richard & Kahler, with a capacity of only 6 barrels per day.

Mr. G. Harpstrite purchased the brewery, in 1859, and soon after formed a co-partnership with Mr. Schlauderman, and continued the business in the old building until 1866, when they erected the present building and occupied the same. The new building is 70x28 ft, five stories in hight, with very deep and capacious cellars. An additional building 40x75 ft., is connected with the brewery, and is used for an ice house, and there is put up by the proprietors, 100,000 tons of ice, annually. The full capacity of the brewery at present is 65 bbls. per day. About 4,000 bbls. of beer is produced, annually, using 10,000 bushels of malt. The beer made here has a wide reputation on account of its superior qualities; and a large amount is shipped to other points on the railroad.

The old brewery is used for a malt house; the cellars for storing wine, and have a storage capacity of 3,000 barrels. There is about 9 acres of ground connected with the brewery, which is very valuable, on account of its adaptation to the present business purposes. The water is of most excellent quality, and in unlimited quantity.

MARBLE DEALERS.

Strolm & Waggoner, established 1861, as Strolm & Co., and so continued until about 4 years since, when Mr. J. W. Waggoner became a member of the firm, and the business was quietly extended and has continued to increase up to the present time. This firm do a very extensive business, one of the largest in Central Illinois, sending a great deal of work to distant parts of this State and adjoining States. They employ a large force of skillful workmen, and manufacture monuments, head stones, all kinds of furniture tops, and also give special attention to all kinds of iron fence works.

Penniwell, Grindall & Co., established 1866. The members of this firm are all practical workmen. Their trade and reputation is not a local one, such is the character of their work. Their business extends to all parts of the State, and they have frequent orders from adjoining States. There are specimens of work at their establishment that cannot be surpassed for skill and beauty of finish, in the United States.

HARDWARE.

Morehouse & Wells commenced the hardware business in the store they now occupy, No. 7 East Main Street, thirteen years ago, and now have a large and prosperous trade. Their stock of hardware, stoves, iron, tinware, belting, wagon wood work, paints, oils, and farming tools, is large and complete. Buying for cash, direct from importers and manufacturers, they are enabled to supply their wholesale customers with the same quality of goods that they are daily handling in their retail trade, at prices comparing favorably with St. Louis or Chicago. Instead of mentioning the fact of their being the oldest established hardware house in the city, and of the large amount of goods sold in the past, this firm seem to have an eye on the future, and to expect success only as they continue to meet the wants of their customers with goods of good quality and at low prices.

Close & Griswold. This firm was originally Close, Griswold & Co., established five years ago. Starting at a time of great competition, and although there were other and longer established houses here at the time, they now rank equal to any other hardware house in the city. This house deals very largely in furnaces adapted to public and private buildings, suitable for burning soft coal. Also, stoves of great variety. They keep a large variety of wagon stocks, and every description of shelf goods and agricultural implements, which they offer for cash at low figures

R. C. Crocker, dealer in hardware, stoves, nails, &c., successor to F. J. Taylor, one of the oldest established hardware houses in Decatur, occupying the same stand where first started. Mr. Crocker but recently succeeded the firm, and has already secured the confidence of the patrons of the old house. Most of the employees of the former proprietor have been retained, including Mr. Wood, one of the most popular and reliable salesmen and efficient bookkeepers in the city.

DRY GOODS.

Decatur, Illinois, is acknowledged as a lively, go-ahead, thriving business city, by all visitors from different sections of our country. As a Chicagoan said, Decatur merchants are "bound to sell" goods, which fact accounts for the establishment of wholesale dry goods houses, which have become permanent institutions within the past few years. Among the foremost, and as pioneers in the trade, stands S. D. Ludden, of the firm of S. D. Ludden & Co., No. 13 East Main Street, who, with James Forrester, opened the wholesale dry goods house in Jno. Ulrich's new block, in July, 1868. After two-and-a-half years of successful trade, the firm of Forrester & Ludden dissolved, January 1, 1871, and in April following the new firm of S. D. Ludden & Co., opened their store at No. 13. East Main Street, as wholesale and retail dealers in dry goods and notions. Mr. Ludden's perfect knowledge of the dry goods business, his long acquaintance with the best merchants of the eastern States, and especially in New York city, as well as in Philadelphia and Boston, is the key which unlocks the mystery of success. For, to be able to make good purchases, a good acquaintance becomes necessary. It is a maxim that "a good purchase is easily sold" The firm of S. D. Ludden & Co., have the abilities and requirements necessary to a successful career before a discriminating public, and that same public is not slow in appreciating the many inducements offered to them.

Jas. Forrester, of J. F. & Co., formerly of N. Y. City, where he has been in the importing commission business, and for the last 12 years in business on his own account, as Trevier & Forester, & Jas. Forester & Co. Mr. Raulet, of this firm, was formerly with J. F. & Co., of N. Y. Mr. F. has been located here for the past three years, where, with his long experience in the dry goods business, with his unusual facilities for buying goods cheap, besides the large business of old customers who formerly traded with him in New York, they have succeeded in building up a prosperous business in the jobbing trade. The store is conveniently arranged for business, having three distinct departments. The 1st floor Retail Room ; 2d floor for Blankets, Shawls, &c., 3d floor 40x80 as Jobbing Room. Their business is constantly increasing ; the sales this year will amount to nearly $200,000.

Thos. A. Gehrman, dealer in American and Foreign Dry Goods, Millinery, &c., keeps his establishment always full, and of the latest style, from the finest to the cheapest in quality. This establishment is one of the most reliable places of business in Decatur, and the business of the house is rapidly increasing, and it is the aim of the proprietor to hold his present regular and extensive trade, by low prices and fair dealing.

"REVOLUTION" DOLLAR STORE.

Kirkman & Co., recently started, are men of extensive business experience, and giving special attention to this popular system for sale of Fancy Goods of every description and variety, and nothing in price above one dollar. Every one should call at this popular resort for bargains.

GROCERIES.

L. B. C. Leffingwell, dealer in Provisions and Staple and Fancy Groceries, No. 9 South Water Street. Mr. Leffingwell has been in the grocery business for five years, most of the time at his present well known stand. He is perfectly reliable, and gives you the worth of your money every time. He is now doing a large business.

H. Lyon, formerly Lyon & Masterman, dealer in Groceries and Produce, started in business here, 1868. All kinds country produce bought, and the higest cash price paid for the same. Mr. Lyon keeps constantly on hand a large stock of foreign and domestic groceries, fine fruits and flour, at the lowest market prices.

LAMPS AND LAMP GOODS.

G. Wallace, well known as the "Non-Explosive Petrolium Fluid Man." He makes a speciality of Danforth's Petrolium Fluid, a new article of Petrolium Oil. It gives a clear light, far preferable and cheaper than the best gas. Mr. Wallace deals in all styles of lamps and lamp goods. Store is No. 14, Central Block.

GAS FITTING.

Mr. J. W. Butman, the efficient Superintendent of the "Decatur Gas Light and Coke Co." has opened an office at No. 5, north side New Square, for the sale of gas and steam pipes, fittings, shades, &c., where he will always be found, unless engaged at the gas works, ready, with experienced workmen, to attend promptly to all orders in his line, and at the lowest city rates. Give him a call, as he guarantees satisfaction.

REAL ESTATE AND INSURANCE.

Warren & Durfee, Real Estate, Title, Abstracts, and General Insurance Ag'ts, are the oldest agents in Macon county, established nearly 15 years. Is the only abstract office, and are the originators and proprietors of the popular continuous and self-corrective system of title abstracts, now extensively used in the Western States.

Kinney & Wuensch, Real Estate and Insurance, have been established about 2 years, making the business of real estate a speciality, and have built up a very large business. They are agents for the North German Lloyd Line, Anchor and Cunard, and several other best European Lines of Steamers.

WHOLESALE LIQUOR HOUSES.

The wholesale liquor house of B. B. Richards is the oldest in Decatur and was established as a wholesale house by the proprietor in 1865. Mr. Richards makes a speciality of pure Kentucky whiskies, and all his selections are made personally, and from a long experience in the business he is enabled to offer the public the best brand of liquors, which will be found at his salcroom, South Main street.

D. W. Brennaman. Established in 1866. Wholesale and retail. Recently enlarged facilities for business with additional room and stock. Mr. Brenneman gives special attention to the wholesale department and offers to the trade one of the largest stocks in the state outside of Chicago, and at prices eqally as low as in Chicago or St. Louis. The character of the goods of this house are strictly No. 1, equal to any found elsewhere.

AGRICULTURAL IMPLEMENTS.

Chambers & Durfee have the largest general stock of farming implements and machinery and garden seeds in central Illinois. They enjoy special facilities in their line, being the representatives of the Decatur Agricultural Works. The members of this firm are able residents of the city, and have contributed much to her present business prosperity, and deserve a good share of public patronage.

Murry & Parks, (originally Parks & Murry,) are the oldest dealers in this line in the city, starting in 1861, and have built up a safe and very extensive trade. Their place of business is in the Priest House block, on North Water street.

C. W. Aiken has been in the business about five years, and besides representing some of the best manufactories of agricultural implements, is himself the inventor and manufacturer of many valuable machines. His warehouse is near the old square.

PORK PACKERS AND BUTCHERS.

Mr. John Imboden was one of the first to engage in the pork packing and butchering trade in this city, begining business here in 1855, and now does the largest pork packing business in the city. He has a large meat market situated over South Main Street, where there can always be found every variety of fresh and pickled meats.

S. G. Effler, dealer in all kinds of fresh and pickled meats, sausage, lard, &c. Mr. Effler has had ten years experience in butchering, formerly with Imboden and has the reputation of furnishing the best quality in the best manner.

Denz & Danzeisen. This firm commenced business in this city two years since; by close attention to the same, with a constant endeavor to furnish their patrons with the best quality of meats and full weights, they have established a good trade and no doubt will retain it.

PHYSICIANS.

Chas. Chenoweth, M. D., dealer in Drugs, Medicines, &c. Mr. Chenoweth is agent for the celebrated California Wine, and San Joaquin Wine Bitters, which are highly recommended by the best physicians of the country, for their purity and peculiar medicinal qualities.

Dr. Barnes, after graduating and receiving the degree of Master of Arts from Dartsmouth College, studied medicine in Philadelphia, and graduated at the Jefferson medical College. During the war he was appointed Surgeon of the 116th Regiment Illinois Volunteers, and served in that capacity until the close of the rebellion, in 1865, when he returned to Decatur, and resumed the practice of medicine with his old partner, under the firm name of Moore & Barnes.

Dr. Moore, the senior partner, graduated in the medical department of the St. Louis University, March, 1853. Commenced the practice of his profession in Carlyle, Clinton county, Ill., the same year, where he remained engaged in the active duties of his profession up to March, 1856, when he removed to Decatur, Illinois, where he has been a leading practitioner ever since. Early in the late war he was appointed Surgeon of the

115th Illinois Vol. Infantry, in which he served with credit to himself and great satisfaction to the Regiment. Soon after entering the army he took high rank as a medical officer, and was placed in charge of the large hospitals at Danville, Kentucky. He shared largely the esteem and confidence of his commanding general.

DENTIST.

Dr. G. T. Shartel, so well known to the residents of Macon county on account of the great success in his profession during his residence in Decatur. With a thorough medical education, he has had extensive experience, secured by a large practice, and avails himself of all the most valuable improvements in his business. The fact of his business constantly increasing is evidences of his reputation, and a due appreciation by the public. Dr. Shartel is prepared to perform work of all kinds, either in mechanical or opperative dentistry.

ATTORNEYS.

The bar of Decatur will compare favorably with that of any other city in the state, and many of its members have a national reputation and have occupied prominent places of public trust. We shall mention but a few of the leading firms of the city :

One of the most prominent firms is Nelson, Roby & Pedagogue, who have had an extensive practice throughout the state, and as they deserve, have the confidence of all who employ them. Mr. Nelson, of this firm, is a member of the present general assembly, and is considered one of its most useful and ablest members and to be one of the rising men of Illinois.

Eden & Oden are considered one of the leading firms of Decatur and have a very large business. Mr. Eden, the senior member of this firm, has practiced in this circuit eighteen years, and has the reputation of being one of the best legal advisers in Illinois. He was a candidate for governor of this state three years since. Mr. Oden, of this firm, has resided here five years and enjoys a reputation for fine abilities as a lawyer.

J. M. Irwin, although not one of the oldest practicing lawyers, yet as a legal adviser he has but few equals at the Decatur bar, and his large increasing practice is evidence of his success.

Bunn & Bunn. This firm is one of considerable talent and deservedly occupy a prominent place at the Decatur bar.

Mr. Ewing. There is no more popular or reliable lawyer in the city, and has a high position among the profession and is doing a good business.

Arthur J. Gallaher, at present judge of the Seventeenth Judicial circuit, and has but few if any superiors at the bar in Illinois. His opinions always sound, and his decisions on matters of constitutional law have given him great prominence throughout this and adjoining states.

CLOCKS AND JEWELRY.

Birely & Abbott, deal extensively in fine jewelry of every description, selected with great care from the largest eastern houses. His stock comprises everything usually kept in a first-class establishment, including the latest, richest, most novel, fashionable jewelry, and silver ware. Particular attention is given to repairing fine jewelry, watches and clocks; and being practical, watch and clock workmen, give this branch personal attention.

BOOT AND SHOE MANUFACTURER AND DEALER.

Geo. F. Wessells is the oldest dealer in the boot and shoe line in the city, having commenced here in 1853. Mr. Wessells' business has been one of steady increase from the begining, and at present he is the largest dealer and has the best selected stock in the city, purchased from the most reliable makers, expressly for city and country trade. Mr. W. is one of the most prominent and valuable citizens, and justly entitled to the position he holds among the business men of Decatur.

BOOKS AND STATIONERY.

D. Espy & Co. This house was first established in 1856, by C. C. Burroughs, who was succeeded by Hostetler & Bro. and T. H. Allen, and in 1870 by the present firm, consisting of D. Espy and Allen Litsenburger. Mr. Litsenburger has resided in Decatur for ten years, and has secured the confidence of the entire community. With the largest and best selected stock in the city in their line, consisting of books, stationery, paper hangings, picture frames, &c. Also agents for Weed's Sewing Machines. And their large and increasing business, with a continuance of the patronage of the old house, shows the high regard held for this firm.

W. E. Wilson. This enterprising and popular house, known by many as the 'Corner Store,' has one of the best stocks of books, stationery, jewelry, and everything usually found in a house of this character. He has also a news depot, where the latest papers and magazines may be found.

DRUGGISTS.

Hubbard & Swearinger have one of the oldest and best drug houses in Decatur. They keep a well selected stock of drugs, chemicals, fancy goods and perfumeries. They give special attention to compounding prescriptions, and at all hours, in the most careful manner.

MUSIC DEALERS.

G. F. Hargis, is one of the oldest dealers in musical instruments in the city. Has always on hand a full supply of Pianos and Organs, by the best makers in the country, including Chickering, Hallut, Davis & Co., and Knabe's Pianos, Mason & Hamlin, and Smith & Co.'s Cabinet Organs. Mr. Hargis also deals in the latest and choicest publications of American and foreign music, and having an able assistant always at his rooms, every one can depend on receiving prompt attention. All orders by mail will be as carefully attended to as if parties were present. Instruments sold by this house are warranted and kept in repair.

Fish & Foster. This firm, favorably known to all lovers of music throughout Macon county, are successors to Lapham & Crissey, and have as large and well selected a stock of music and of all kinds of musical instruments as can be found in Central Illinois. Prof. Foster, of this firm, was formerly connected with one of the largest music houses East, which secures to the firm special facilities in the purchase of their goods, and they give their patrons the benefit of them. Prof. Foster has had ten years experience as a teacher, and he has been recently secured by the Decatur Conservatory of Music, as instructor of vocal music.

BANKERS.

J. Millikin & Co.'s bank was established in 1861. The members of this firm consist of J. Millikin and J. R. Gorin, who are old residents of the city, and always enjoyed the confidence of the community, and rank among the best business men of Decatur. This bank deals largely in foreign exchange, and also gives some attention to real estate loans, and their business done is quite large, and considered perfectly safe.

There are two other banks in Decatur, ore conducted by Peddecord & Burrows, the other by Smiths, Hammer & Co., both doing an extensive business, and their officers are well known business men.

SEWING MACHINES.

William W. Lapham is agent for the celebrated Singer Machines, of which over 40,000 more were sold, in 1870, than any other make, which is of itself the best possible recommendation for the machine.

D. Espy & Co., are agents for the Weed machine. It is one of the most popular machines, being simple in construction, easy to operate, having a straight needle, with perfect feed and tension.

BRAMBLE'S PLEASURE GARDEN.

The popular place of resort, known as Bramble's Pleasure Garden, is owned by W. H. Bramble, Esq., who is an old resident of Decatur, and has always contributed largely to the promotion of public enterprise and welfare of the city. These gardens are located in the southwestern part of the city, and consist of six and one-half acres of ground, possessing natural attractions of a peculiar and romantic character, to which Mr. B. has added many improvements. Among them an attractive building fitted up with handsome parlors, ice cream saloon, also a large bath house, fountains, swings, &c. There is an unfailing spring of the purest water on the grounds, which has been analyzed by Dr. Chenoweth, and found to possess largely properties of a medicinal character. This, together with an abundance of shade trees on the grounds, make it a desirable resort either for sabbath schools, religious societies and other organizations or any private individual. There is no intoxicating liquors or beverage sold or allowed on the grounds. Mr. Bramble's residence, a fine large brick building, is situated on a rising elevation at the west end of the grounds, where any one desiring to spend a few days or weeks in search of health, rest or pleasure, can secure rooms and board, and have the use of the grounds and house. During the winter there is a skating park covering two acres of ground, where all lovers of this delightful pastime can enjoy themselves.

Mr. Bramble has achieved a national reputation by his valuable inventions of "Self-regulating measuring scales," and "Post Office Box."

CROCKERY, GLASSWARE, &C.

R. Liddle, deals in crockery, glassware, and in fact, in almost everything necessary to the complete furnishing of a house, including stoves, tinware, plated ware and cutlery. The crockery and glassware department is distinct from the other, having recently been removed to new and commodious quarters on North Water Street. There is no more attractive store in Decatur. The goods are bought of importers and manufacturers, and in such large quantities that Mr. Liddle secures the largest discounts from regular rates, and is enabled to offer greater inducements in way of prices than smaller houses.

GENERAL AGENTS.

Wood & Montgomery, general insurance and real estate agents, are both men of extensive experience and are deservedly popular. This firm represents many of the largest fire insurance companies in the United States, and which for security and promptness cannot be excelled in the world, representing about $15,000,000 of cash assets. They are also general agents for the Widows' and Orphans' Life Insurance Company, of New York. Besides their extensive insurance business, Messrs. Wood & Montgomery give considerable attention to buying and selling real estate, paying taxes, and all business pertaining to the real estate agency.

Crawford & Griswold are general agents of the Commonwealth Life Insurance Company, of New York. This Co., has already taken the front rank among the best life insurance companies, although among the youngest; and as evidence of its purpose to maintain this position, it has already chosen as President Mr. Seth E. Thomas, whose name is a favorite household word, associated as it is with the popular and reliable Seth Thomas Clocks. "Its directors embrace some of the ablest, strongest and most active business men in the community," says the New York *Independent*. Mr. Morse, its Vice President, is a graduate of a life office, and is exactly fitted for this position. Mr. Homes, Secretary and Actuary, is from the New York State Insurance Department, and recently resigned to take this place. We give some of the features of this Company: All cash; non-forfeiture incontestable from date; no restrictions on travel or occupation; 30 days' grace allowed. It has established a Decatur Branch, with the following officers:

OFFICERS.

Wm. L. Hammer	President
Geo. Priest	Vice President
A. P. Griswold	Secretary
R. P. Lytle,	
J. A. Aikman, M. D.,	Ex. Com.
A. A. Murray,	
Crea & Ewing	Attorneys
B. F. Sibley, M. D.,	Med. Examiners
J. A. Aikman, M. D.,	
Smiths, Hammer, & Co	Bankers

MANAGERS.—Wm. L. Hammer, C. C Burroughs, Virgil H. Park, E. A. Gastman, A. P. Griswold, Charles A. Ewing,

Robert P. Lytle, Wm. H. Harris, Wm. Lintner, George Priest, A. A. Murray, Walter J. Taylor, J. A. Aikman, M. D., Benj. F. Sibley, M. D.

CLAIM AGENT

C. H. Fuller, Esq., is one of the oldest and most reliable U. S. military claim agents in the city. Mr. Fuller gives careful attention to collecting all military claims, whether for horse claims, prize money, bounty, or back pay, and makes no charges unless claims are allowed. He is also Notary Public, and from his long residence, and having been extensively engaged in business, and holding many places of public trust, is enabled to protect and further the interests of all who do business with him. Mr. F. is one of the most active and public spirited citizens of Decatur.

PATENT SOLICITOR.

Chas. P. Housum, solicitor of patents, and agent for the sale of patents, has built up quite a large and successful business, and gives satisfaction to all who are fortunate in securing his services.

LIVERY STABLE.

A. W. Hardy has the best and largest Livery and Feed Stables in Decatur, and has some of the finest teams to be found in the State. The stock is all first class, and patrons will not be overcharged for hire. They have special accommodations for farmers, for feeding and stabling.

UNDERTAKER.

Daniel Aungst, undertaker, and dealer in coffins, metalic burial cases and caskets. Has the best and most extensive assortment ever kept in the city. Mr. Aungst has arrangements for preserving a corpse natural for any length of time necessary, until day of burial, without additional cost to his patrons.

CARPETS AND WALL PAPER.

Messrs. Abel & Lock, are the oldest exclusive carpet, wall paper and furnishing house in Decatur. They have a fine assortment of carpets of foreign and American manufacture, a good line of window shades and fixtures, and wall paper of every description. These gentlemen thoroughly understand their business, giving personal attention to the same, and having able assistants, warrant all their work, and are deservedly quite popular.

DECATUR INFIRMARY.

Drs. M. & H. Brandom, the "Twin Brothers," have established in this city their Infirmary for treatment of all diseases relating to the Eye and Ear. It has become the resort of multitudes from different parts of the State, who seek relief for these organs, and who almost invariably are fully restored. Their treatment is considered superior to any other known or practiced, and used with perfect safety in all cases. Some of their cures have been truly wonderful, and a visit to their Infirmary will convince the greatest skeptic these statements are real facts.

CLOTHING, FURNISHING GOODS.

J. R. Race & Co., have the largest establishment in Illinois outside of Chicago, and offer equal inducements to any in that city. Messrs. Race & Co. are extensive jobbers in jeans, flannels, yarns, &c., having the productions of several large woolen establishments, and besides a very large stock of ready made clothing and furnishing goods they have a complete merchant tailoring department, under one roof and in one of the finest business houses in the city. The trade of this firm extends to all parts of the state and is quite large and constantly increasing.

ICE AND WOOD DEALERS.

Martin Fortsmeyer, Esq., has very complete and extensive arrangements for supplying the city with ice and wood of the best quality and at low rates. Mr. F. has resided here over 15 years and been closely identified with the public welfare most of the time, is a good representative of the American workingmen, beginning in business here with no capital but stout, honest hands and heart, he has amassed considerable property and has occupied and still holds several places of prominent public trust, and enjoys the confidence of the people of the city and county.

HOTELS.

Priest House—This is one of the oldest and best hotels in the city. The proprietor, Frank Priest, has kept the house for several years. It is centrally located and sufficiently retired for comfort and convenience of its guests, and enjoys a good reputation among the traveling public for accommodation and prices. A free omnibus is run to and from all regular trains.

St. Nicholas—Laux Brothers, proprietors. This house is located on the southwest corner of the old square, and has recently been enlarged by additional building, and is much improved and has first class accommodations, including a large sample room, parlors and reading rooms. There is also a good livery stable connected with the house, and a free omnibus runs to and from all trains. The Laux Brothers have been brought up to the hotel business from boys, and are enabled, by long experience and personal attention to their business, to meet all the expectations and wants of their guests. Their table is always supplied with the best of the market, and served in a manner to suit the most fastidious. The sleeping accommodations are excellent, special attention being given to the cleanliness of the same. The hotel is deservedly one of the most popular in central Illinois.

Hockaday House, located near the new square, is nearly new; everything is in good condition, and clean, and all the conveniencies usually found in a good hotel.

BUSINESS DIRECTORY,

ARRANGED ACCORDING TO THEIR VARIOUS BUSINESS PURSUITS.

Abstract Makers.

WARREN & DURFEE, Central Block.

Agents, Insurance.

CRAWFORD & GRISWOLD, cor. Water and East Main.
KINNEY & WUENSCH, Opera House Block.
TIBBETTS, SAMUEL, 14 south side New Square.
WARREN & DURFEE, Central Block.
WOOD & MONTGOMERY, 8 Powers' Block.

Agents, Real Estate.

KINNEY & WUENSCH, Smith's Opera House Block.
WARREN & DURFEE, Central Block.
WOOD & MONTGOMERY, 8 Power's Block.

Agent, U. S. Claim.

FULLER, C. H., Council Rooms.

Artists.

Moeller, Rudolph, 24 Main St., up Stairs.
LAPHAM, A. MILT., Opera House Block.

Attorneys at Law.

BUCKINGHAM, I. A., 6 s s New Square up stairs.
BUNN & BUNN, 13 E. Main
CREA & EWING, Powers' Block, East Main.
EDEN & ODOR, N. Water.
Emerson, Albert, 12 E. Main.
GREER, SAMUEL F., Court House.
IRWIN, JAMES M., 18 Merchant St.
JOHNS, W. C., 24 E. Main.
Jones, Paul F., 5 Powers' Block.
Lake, J. C., cor. State and New Square.

LEE, THOMAS, over J. Millikin & Co's Bank.
McComas, Charles C., over Smiths, Hammer & Co.'s Bank.
Murphy, F. S., 24 E. Main.
NELSON, ROBY & PEDDECORD, 4 New Square, up stairs.
PARK, EDWIN, over J. Millikin & Co.'s Bank.
Parmelee, Harlan P., cor. N. State and New Square.
POST & BUCKINGHAM, 23 N. Water Street.
Smith & Sterrett, 22 N. Water.

Auction and Commission Merchants.

Thompson & Co., 1 w s Old Square.

Agricultural Implements, etc.

AIKEN, C. W., Prairie, new square.
CHAMBERS & DURFEE. 16 Main st.
HAWORTH & SONS, n w cor. Cerro Gordo and Morgan sts.
MURRAY & PARK, 21 Main st.

Bakers and Confectioners.

Bailey, A. 19 Main st.
Miller, C., No. 6 Water st.

Bankers.

MILLIKIN, J., & Co., No. 11 Main st.
Peddecord & Burrows, 4 New Square.
Smiths, Hammer & Co., cor. N. Water and New Square.

Barbers.

Ansback, Gus., 16 New Square.
Fell, Louis, 8 Merchant st.
Jacobs, Chas., under Priest's Hotel.
Stewart & Rogan, 8 E. Main.
Young & Norman, 6 N. Water.

Billiard Saloons.

CAIN & ANDREWS, St. Nicholas Hotel.
MILLS, E. H., 7 n w cor. Old Square.
PRIEST'S HOTEL, Priest's block.

Bill Poster.

FRANK HAINES, Fish & Foster's music store.

Blacksmiths.

Kit Karson & Kramer, W. Main, near church.
GAHMAN & WICKS, cor. N. Water and Cerro Gordo sts.
Hamsher & Son, 24 Mason st.
Thomas Hughes, cor. Prairie and Broadway.
Nichols & Foose, 43 E. Main.

Bottler of Ale and Beer.

KUNZ, FRED., cor. Main and Jackson.

Boots and Shoes.

Adams, E. G., 16 Merchant sts.
Busher, W. F., & Co., 15 Main st.
Eger, L., 17 Main st.
Hamsbuger, G., & Co., Fenton's block, N. Water st.
Powers, Ferris & Co., 18 E. Main.
Rugg & Moore, 10 Main st.
Geo. Snelser, 38 E. Main st.
SMELSLEY & Co., 36 Main st.
WESSELLS, GEO. F., 15 N. Water st.

Books and Stationery.

Alliu & Hostkler, 9 E. Main st.
ESPY, D., & Co., 17 E. Main st.
BRAMBLE, O., & BRO., Postoffice building.
WILSON, W. E., n w cor. E. Main and Water sts.

Brewery.

Harpsrite & Schladerman, s e city limits.
Weber, Nicholas, on I. C. R. R., S.

Brick Yards.

Howenstein, John, n of city limits.
Myers & Brant, S. Broadway cor. Malone st.
Whitmer, H. W. res. S. Broadway.

Butchers.

BLENZ & DANZEISER, 3 Old Square.
Dresbach, A. J., E. Eldorado, n Front .
IMBODEN, J., & Co., cor. S. Main and Wood sts.
Weitsel & Adams, cor. Cerro Gordo and Broadway.

Carpenters.

Lehman, John A , 87 N. Water.
Lyon, G. S., N. Eldorado and Pine sts.
Martin & Williams, Jefferson between Church and Union sts.
Mills & Harry, 69 N. Water.
Shockley, D. C., s e cor. N. Water and Cerro Gordo sts.

Carriage Makers.

GAHMAN & WICKS, cor. N. Water and Cerro Gorda sts.
Taylor & Bradley, W. Main near Church sts.

Carpets, Etc.

Abel & Locke, 34 E. Main st.
QUINLAN, W. J., & BRO., 24 E. Main.

Cigars and Tobacco.

KEPLER, A., s e cor. Old Square.
Michl Joseph, & Co., 12 N. Water st.
Osmers, John, 29 N. Water st.
Young & Norman, 6 N. Water st.

Clothing.

BARNEY, J. S., 27 N. Water st.
Ehrman, I. W., 22 E. Main st.
FENTON, J. L., & Co., 23 N. Water st.
RACE, J. R., & Co., 17 N. Water st.
SMALLWOOD & HUDSON, 28 E. Main st.
Stine, B., Central block, Old Square
Zekind, A. M., & Co., 32 E. Main st.

Commission Merchants.

Bills & Hardy, Old Revere House building.

Coal Dealers.

GAHMAN & WICKS, cor. Water and Cerro Gordo sts.
Western Coal Co., N. Franklin and R. R. crossing.

Confectioners.

BRAMBLE, O., & BRO., P. O. Building.
Cassell, John, Prairie and N. Water sts.
HILL, A. F., 26 Merchant st
Smith, L. J., 62 Main st.

Coopers.

Litterer, Martin D., Morgan st and T. W, & W. R. R.
Pitcher, J. L., Mason st e of Old Custom Mills.
Rusk & Bro., s of Priest's Mill.

Crockery, China, Glassware, &c., &c.,

CLARK, J. S., & Co., 4 N. Water.

Crockery and Tile Factory.

Traver, William, W. Main bet. College and Pine.

Decatur Gas Light & Coke Co.

Ewing, F. N., President; J. K. Warren, secretary and treasurer. Executive committee—F. N. Ewing, L. Burrows, J. K. Warren. Superintendent, J. W. Britman, office n. side New Square, No. 5.

Dentists.

Cochrane, A., N. Water st., w of New Square
CORMAN, O. F., cor. Main and Merchant sts.
DAWKINS, R. C., over Smiths, Hammer & Co.'s bank.
Lukens, E., over Stoner's drug store.
SHARTEL, G. T., cor. E. Main and Merchant sts.

Druggists.

CHENOWETH, C., 80 Merchant st.
Gardiner, J. M., 12 Main st.
HAND, J. S., & Co., 19 N. Water st.
Hildebrandt, Theo., 6 New Square.
HUBBARD & SWEARINGER, cor. E. Main and N. Water sts.
Roberts & Armstrong, 8 E. Main st.
STONER, A. J., 14 south side of New Square.

Dry Goods.

Bruce, G. M., 13 N. Water st.
FORRESTER, JAMES, & Co., 8 Merchant st.
Hays & Bruce, 25 N. Water st.
Linn & Scruggs, 2 and 4 Merchant st.
LUDDEN, S. D., & Co., 13 E. Main st.
RACE, J. R. & Co., 17 N. Water st.
Roach & McReynolds, cor. N. State and New Square.
Ruth, A , & Co., 10 Merchant st.

Engine Builders.

BURROUGHS & CO., William and Morgan

Express Companies.

AMERICAN, Main and Old Square.
UNITED STATES, Main and Old Square.

Fire Kindler.

KING, J. B., manufacturer, 25 W. Eldorado.

Flouring Mills.

ILLINOIS CENTRAL, Geo. Priest, cor. Water and Broadway.
McDonald, J., near R. R. crossing.
Shellabarger Mills, D. S. Shellabarger & Co., N. Water and T. W. & W. R. R.
St. Clair Mills, J. M. Rainey & Co., N. T. W. & W. R. R. and Water.

Foundry.

CENTRAL IRON WORKS, William and Morgan.

Furnishing Goods.

KEELER, S. T., 24 Merchant.

Furniture.

BUTZIN, FREDERICK, 52 E. Main.
Drake & Bro., 6 N. Water and R R. crossing.
LINTNER, WM. & CO , factory corner Morgan and William, salesroom 8 s s New Square.

Gas Fitting.

BUTMAN, J. W., 5 n s New Square.

Grocers.

Adderly Geo., N. Water and R. R. crossing.
Bally, B. C., N. Broadway and Mason.
Baker & Jack, cor. Main and Water.
Barnett, D. M., 5 n s New Square.
CLEAVELAND, M. A., 22 Merchant st.
Gill, L. M. & Co., 10 New Square.
Henry, E. & Co., N. Broadway, bet. Eldorado and Cerro Gordo.
Imboden, A. H., 21 S. Main.
LEFFINGWELL, L. B C., 9 S. Main.
Leiby, Jacob & Son, 14 E. Main.
Luthen, Joseph, 36 Morgan.
Lewis, H. B. & Bro., cor. Morgan and Cerro Gordo.
LYON, H., 28 Merchant st.
McEvoy, J., opp. R. R Depot.
McRoberts, John, s. e cor. Square and 8 N. Franklin.
Milligan & Skelley, 22 N. Franklin.
Newell & Hammer, 11 N. Water.
Niedermeyer & Corson, 21 N. Water.
Reeme, Wm. H., 41 N. Water.
Reployle & Co., Central Block, Old Square.
W. S. Roby, N. Water nr. R. R. crossing.
Smith, S. D., 2 Priest's Block.

SHUPP, SAMUEL, 17 N. Main st.
STRAILY, S. M., 20 Main st.
Skelley, Frank, 30 W. Eldorado st.
ULLRICH, J & Co., 6 Merchant st.
Williams, John R., res. N. Main and Green.

Grain Dealer.

HAWORTH, M., n w cor. Cerro Gordo and Morgan.

Gun Smith.

Mueller, H., 36 E. Main st.

Hall.

Marble, J. R. Race & Co., 17 N. Water.

Hardware, &c.

CLOSS & GRISWOLD, 30 Main st.
CROCKER, RUFUS & Co., 9 N. Water.
Liddle, R., s e cor. New Square.
MOREHOUSE & WELLS, 7 E. Main st.
Taylor, F. J., 9 N. Water st.

Hats and Caps.

FENTON, J. L., & Co., 23 N. Water st.
KEELER, S. T., 24 Merchant st.
RACE. J. R., & Co., 17 N. Water st.
SMALLWOOD & HUDSON, 28 E. Main st.
Stine, B., Central block, Old Square.
Zekind, A. M., & Co., 32 E. Main st.

Hides, Tallow, Rags, &c.

STUTSMAN, J., 2 E. Main.

Hotels.

Franklin House, Colorado and Broadway.
Frederick Harris, Morgan and E. Eldorado.
HOCKADAY HOUSE, s e cor. Merchant and E. Prairie sts.
McEVOY, JOHN, Front and E. Cerro Gordo.
MORONY, J. J., Front bet. E. Cerro Gordo and E. Eldorado.
National Hotel, opp. R. R. Depot.
Pennsylvania House, n. w cor. Water and E. Main.
Planter's House, E. Eldorado and Front.
PRIEST HOTEL, n w cor. Old Square and N. Main.
St. Charles Hotel, E. North and Jackson.
Sherman House, E. William st.
ST. NICHOLAS HOTEL, s w cor. Main and Old Square.
Union House, E. Main bet. Jackson and Franklin.

House Furnishing Goods.

Liddle, R., 22 and 24 New Square.

Hubs, Spokes, Felloes, &c.

CLOSE & GRISWOLD, 30 E. Main.

Ice and Wood.

FORTSMEYER, MARTIN, s w cor. W. Main and Church.

Iron Works.

CENTRAL IRON WORKS. cor. William and Morgan.

Jewelry.

BIRELY & ABBOTT, 9 E. Main.
BRAMBLE, O., & BRO., P. O. building.
Lilleston, S. D., 17 E. Main.
WILSON, W. E., n w cor. E. Main and N. Water,

Job Printers.

ADDIS, W. H., Opera House block.
MOSSER & HAMSHER, cor. Main and Water.
SHOAFF & MILLER, Opera House block.

Justices of the Peace.

Goodman, George, 7 Powers block.
HATCH, M. K., Council Rooms, cor. E. Main and Water.
Steel, Samuel, over Smiths, Hammer & Co.'s bank.

Knitting Machine.

LAMB KNITTING MACHINE, 10 N. Water.

Ladies' Dress Trimmings.

Maxwell, W. M., 10 N. Water.

Lamps, Oils, &c.

WALLACE, G., Central Block.

Livery and Sale Stables.

CALDWELL BROS., Main, rear of St. Nicholas Hotel.
HARDY, A. W., s e cor. New Square and N. Franklin.
Mason & Culp, 6 Main.

Linseed Oil Manufacturers.

Sawyer, W. & B., cor. E. Main and S. Broadway.

Lumber Yards.

Elwood & Co., Eldorado and I. C. R. R. crossing.
Foster, H. E., 34 Mason.
Stare & Bro., cor. Franklin and Cerro Gordo.

Swingley, S. K., N. Water and R. R. crossing.

Machinists.

BURROUGHS & Co., cor. William and Morgan.

Marble Works.

BARRETT, W. M., & CO., cor. N. Main and Prairie.
CITY MARBLE WORKS, cor. E. Main and Franklin.
Peniwell, Grindol & Co., cor. E. Main and Franklin.
STROHM & WAGGONER, cor. N. Water and New Square.

City Marshal.

HAWORTH, JOHN, Council Rooms.

Deputy City Marshal.

MORONY, ANTHONY, Council Rooms.

Meat Markets.

EPPLER, S. G , 19 N. Main.
Whitsel & Adams, s w cor. Broadway and Cerro Gordo.

Millinery.

Gehrmann, Theo. A., 12 Merchant.
HICKMAN, MRS. D. C., Opera House block.
MILLER, MISS ANNIE, 20 Merchant.
Steward, Mrs. C., 30 N. Water.
Waterman & Muhleman, Misses, cor. E. Main and Merchant.

Milk Dealers.

Maffit. D. A.
Taylor, Benj. F., Fair Grounds.

News Dealers.

BRAMBLE, O., & BRO., P. O. building.
Crissey, W. E., 9 E. Main.
Dogget, R., Old P. O.
ESPY, D., & CO., 17 E. Main.
WILSON, W. E., n w cor. E. Main and N. Water.

Newspapers.

DAILY AND WEEKLY DEMOCRAT, Opera House Block.
DECATUR GAZETTE AND CHRONI-CLE, 14 E. Main.
DECATUR WEEKLY REPUBLICAN, n e cor. Court House Block.

ILLINOIS VOLKSBLATT, 14 Main.
MAGNET, Opera House Block.

Notaries Public.

FULLER, C. H., Council Rooms.
WUENSCH, ALFRED, Opera House Block.

Notions and Varieties.

Clark, E. M., N. Water and E. Prairie.
Reeme, J. W., 32 Merchant st.

Occulists and Aurists,

BRANDOM, M. & H., 19 N. Water, up stairs.

Paint Shop.

Gilbert, J. E., 26 Merchant st.

Paints, Oils, &c.

CLOSE & GRISWOLD, 30 E. Main.

Patent Solicitor.

HOUSUM, C. P., 11 Power's Block.

Photographers.

Barnwell, E. A., 27 N. Water, up stairs.
BUTLER, T. H., over Smiths, Hammer & Co.'s Bank.
LAPHAM, A. MILT., 15 E. Main st.

Photographers.

PITNER, W. C., 17 N. Water, up stairs.
Laforgee, Marion, bds Hockaday House.
Scibird, H. W., 12 E. Main.

Physicians.

Allison, B. A., Central Block.
Brown & Parker, cor. Main and Water.
CHENOWETH, C., 30 Merchant.
Durr, —, cor. Franklin and N. Water.
Hostetler, J. H., 10 N. Water, 2d floor.
HOSTETLER, W. B., 8 E. Main, over Roberts and Armstrong's drug store.
May, P., n e cor. William and Franklin.
McBride, S., 6 New Square, up stairs.
McMillin, G. W., 8 E. Main.
Moore & Barnes, cor. E. Main and N. Water.
Randall, J. N., 12 E. Main.
ROUTH, JAMES W., 22 Merchant.
SIBLEY, B. F., 6 Council Building.
STONER, A. J., 14 S. Side New Square.
Wilson, W. E., n w cor. E. Main and Water.

Pianos and Organs.

Hargis, G. F., over Espy & Co.'s store.

7

Murphy, R. H., over Wilson's store.
Fish & Foster, 10 N. Water.

Pictures, Frames, &c.

ESPY, D., & Co., 17 E. Main.
LAPHAM, A. MILT, Oper House Block.

Pleasure Garden.

BRAMBLE'S PLEASURE GARDEN, S.
E. Church st.

Produce, &c.

Holden, Charles L., 28 N. Water.

Pump Factory.

Lintner, Wm., E. William opp. Morgan.

Restaurants.

HILL, A. F., 26 Merchant.
MILLS, E. H., 7 cor. Old Square.

Revolution Dollar Store.

KIRKMAN & Co., 18 Merchant.

Rolling Mill.

Harris, W. H., Supt., e of R. R. Depot.

Saddles, Harness, &c.

Hamsher, D., Central Block.
HAMSHER, JOHN, 18 S. side New
Square.
Starr, J. G., & Son, 8 W. side Old
Square.

Saloons.

Phillip Honecker, res. 92 S. Broadway.
CAIN & ANDREWS, St. Nicholas Hotel.
Concordia Saloon, S. Main nr Wood.
CRYSTAL PALCE, 4 E. Main.
DALEY, JAMES, Front and E. Cerro
Gordo.
Duggan, Michael, Front nr Eldorado.
Exchange, 6 E. Main.
Farner, Louis, 8 N. Franklin.
HACKETT & BARR, Opera House
Block.
Hubbard & Bro., P. O. Building.
Carroll, Michael, n c cor. Eldorado and
Broadway.

Prairie, bet. Merchant and N. Water.
Reid, Wm. Front, nr Cerro Gordo.
Wiefel, Charles, cor. S. Water and E.
Main.

Sash and Blind Factories.

Elwood D., & Co., Eldorado and I. C.
R. R.
Stare & Bro., cor. Cerro Gordo and
Franklin.

Sewing Machines.

Grover & Baker, Miss A Miller.
SINGER, 10 N. Water.
Espy, D., & Co., Agts., 17 E. Main.
Wheeler & Wilson, Abel & Locke, Water and Main.

Shoemakers.

McClure, Festus, w. side N. Water bet.
Cerro Gordo and Mason.
Winholtz, Wm., 33 Morgan.

Skating Rink.

BRAMBLE'S, S. E. Church.

Soda Manufacturer.

KUNZ, FRED., cor. E. Main and Jackson.

Stoves, Tinware, &c.

Carter, C. A., W. side Old Square nr. W.
Main.
CLOSE & GRISWOLD, 30 E. Main.
CROCKER, RUFUS C., 9 N. Water.
MOREHOUSE & WELLS, 7 E. Main.

Merchant Tailors.

BARNEY, J. S., 27 N. Water.
Bachman, Geo., E. Main nr Franklin.
RACE, J. R., & Co., 17 N. Water.
SMALLWOOD & HUDSON, 28 E. Main.

Telegraph Companies.

GREAT WESTERN, 15 E. Main.
Western Union, 34 E. Main, up stairs.

Toys, Notions, and Fancy Goods.

ESPY, D., & Co., 17 E. Main.

Trimmings, Paper Patterns, &c.

Maxwell, Wm. M., 10 N. Water.

Trunks, Valises, &c.

FENTON, J. L., & Co., 23 N. Water.

Undertakers.

AUNGST, DANIEL, 6 s side Old Square.
BUTZIN, FRED., 52 E. Main.
Givler, M. Y., n e cor. Old Square.
Scudder, W. W., 5 Old Square.

Vegetables, Fruits, Meats, Game, &c.

BLOCK, S., 3 Opera House Block.

Vinegar Factory.

Smick, E. A., S. Main.

Wagon Makers.

Athen, Joseph, W. Main nr Church.
Cramer & McClelland, 37 E. Main.
GAHMAN & WICKS, cor. N. Water and
Cerro Gordo.
HAMSHER & SON, 24 Mason.

HEBENSTREIT, A., Jackson.

Wall Paper.

Abel & Locke, 34 E. Main.
ESPY, D., & CO., 17 E. Main.

Wines, Liquors, &c.

BRENNEMAN, D. W., 20 and 22 s side
City Park.
CASSELL, BERRY H., 26 E. Main.
Dodson, Benj. F., 14 Merchant.
HACKETT & BARR, Opera House
Block.
RICHARDS, B. B., 11 Main.

Woolen Goods.

BOYD, HASKELL & CO., cor. Mason
and Broadway.

Woolen Mill.

DECATUR WOOLEN MILL, cor. Mason and Broadway.

www.ingramcontent.com/pod-product-compliance
Lightning Source LLC
Chambersburg PA
CBHW021641270326
41931CB00008B/1115